# FEEDING

# In Memory of Robert A. Calvert

# FEEDING THE WOLF

## John B. Rayner
## and the Politics of Race,
## 1850–1918

Gregg Cantrell
*University of North Texas*

A John Wiley & Sons, Ltd., Publication

*Registered Office*
John Wiley & Sons, Ltd, The Atrium, Southern Gate, Chichester, West Sussex,
PO19 8SQ, UK
*Editorial Offices*
350 Main Street, Malden, MA 02148-5020, USA
9600 Garsington Road, Oxford, OX4 2DQ, UK
The Atrium, Southern Gate, Chichester, West Sussex, PO19 8SQ, UK

For details of our global editorial offices, for customer services, and for
information about how to apply for permission to reuse the copyright material
in this book please see our website at www.wiley.com/wiley-blackwell.

***Library of Congress Cataloging-in-Publication Data***

Cantrell, Gregg, 1958-
Feeding the wolf: John B. Rayner and the politics of race, 1850-1918/Gregg
Cantrell.
    p. cm.
An abridged and rev. version of: Kenneth and John B. Rayner and the limits of
southern dissent/Gregg Cantrell.
    Includes index.
    ISBN 978-0-88295-961-0 (alk. paper)
    1. Rayner, John B., 1850-1918. 2. Afro-American politicians—Texas-Biography. 3.
Politicians—Texas—Biography. 4. Texas—Politics and government—1865-1950. 5.
Populism—Texas—History. 6. Texas—Race relations. 7. Afro-Americans—Texas—
Politics and government. 8. Racism—Political aspects—Texas—History. 9. Reconstruc-
tion—Texas. I. Cantrell, Greg, 1958- Kenneth and John B. Rayner and the limits of
Southern dissent. II. Title.

F391.R36 C36 2001
976.4'061'092—dc21                                                                                    00-050835
{B}

# Contents

# INTRODUCTION
## AND ACKNOWLEDGMENTS

This book is an abridged and revised version of an earlier work, *Kenneth and John B. Rayner and the Limits of Southern Dissent,* published in 1993 by the University of Illinois Press. That book told the story of John B. Rayner, the black Populist leader and educator of Texas, and his father, Kenneth Rayner, the powerful North Carolina politician and slaveholder. When I wrote the original book I debated the question of publishing it as two separate biographies. Both Rayners deserved a biography, and neither had ever been the subject of a book-length inquiry. Both were men of enormous intelligence and ability, although the circumstances of their births (the younger Rayner was either one-eighth or one-sixteenth African American) dictated that they would lead very different lives. Despite this, each forged his own important career as a political maverick who dared to challenge the Democratic Party and the South's racial orthodoxy. And each, in his own way, paid the price that the South exacted from those who crossed the permissible boundaries of dissent. The parallels and the ironies in their public careers convinced me that their fascinating stories needed telling together, and I am glad that I did that.

However, I also knew that joining the father and son in a multigenerational biography would limit the audience I would reach. In American colleges and universities the United States history survey is almost always divided at the end of Reconstruction—just as Kenneth

Rayner's career was ending and John B. Rayner's was beginning. In upper-level southern history courses the division is similar: most departments offer separate classes in the Old South and New South. Only half of my book would be deemed appropriate for any of these courses. Moreover, an instructor in an African American History course was not likely to assign a book that was half "white" biography and half "black" biography. Nor would one teaching a course in Texas history assign a book whose first half takes place in North Carolina, and vice-versa.

Of my two subjects, John B. Rayner is in many ways the more compelling. No other African American Populist has ever been the subject of a biography. Indeed, beyond Booker T. Washington, very few black political leaders from the turn-of-the-century South have received biographical scrutiny. This comes as no great surprise, given the extent to which the opportunities and aspirations of African Americans were circumscribed during that terrible era in American race relations.

John B. Rayner's story—sometimes triumphant, occasionally shameful, mostly tragic—has much to tell us about that era. His early experiences as a local Republican officeholder in the 1870s illustrate many of the contradictory features of America's "unfinished revolution," as historian Eric Foner has aptly called Reconstruction. Rayner's rise to prominence as an orator, organizer, and political strategist for the Texas People's Party in the 1890s illuminates what Populist scholars Lawrence Goodwyn and Gene Clanton respectively have described as the "democratic promise" and the "humane preference" of the agrarian movement, while simultaneously showing the limitations of Populism's politics of inclusion. Finally, Rayner's zigzag course after 1900 shows us the nearly impossible position that talented, politically active African Americans found themselves in during the age of Jim Crow, as he tried to function both as a Booker T. Washington-style accommodationist and as a fighter for continuing black participation in politics. The most famous biography of any Populist, C. Vann Woodward's *Tom Watson,* showed us the tortuous path that white Southern politics took during and after the Populist "moment";

John B. Rayner's life reveals the even more bewildering choices that black politicians confronted during those same years.

I am indebted to Andrew J. Davidson of Harlan Davidson, Inc., for agreeing to publish this volume and for his expert editorial guidance. I also wish to thank the University of Illinois Press for removing copyright obstacles. John B. Rayner first came to my attention some fifteen years ago in a graduate seminar taught by Professor Martin V. Melosi, now of the University of Houston. Over the years that followed, I received valuable input and criticism from Dale T. Knobel, Lawrence Goodwyn, Walter L. Buenger, Worth Robert Miller, D. Scott Barton, August Meier, members of the extensive Rayner family, and many others for whom space precludes specific mention.

This book was researched in archives and libraries from Texas to North Carolina to Washington, D.C., but I owe special thanks to the archivists at Texas A&M University, the University of Texas, Rice University, Baylor University, the University of North Carolina, the Texas State Library, the North Carolina Division of Archives and History, and the Houston Public Library. My wife Brenda Freeman Cantrell was supportive in many ways as I took time away from family responsibilities to work on the manuscript. My boys Drew, Calvin, and Nolan distracted me from writing, for which I am grateful.

But there is one person to whom I owe a special debt. The late Robert A. Calvert of Texas A&M University was the first to make me understand the true significance of that obscure political movement known as Populism. A lifelong champion of the common man and woman, Bob embodied the noblest ideals of Populism. As friend and mentor, he never ceased to believe in me, and this book would not exist without his encouragement. With affection and gratitude, I dedicate it to his memory.

Gregg Cantrell

John B. Rayner

# CHAPTER ONE

# In the Crucible of Reconstruction

FEW GROUPS IN AMERICAN HISTORY have commanded as much popular fascination or scholarly interest as the slaveholding planters of the Old South. They have been admired and reviled, alternately romanticized as a class of men (and women) who built a graceful civilization now "gone with the wind," or debunked as cruel overlords who profited from an institutionalized system of oppression.

As historians have struggled to come to terms with the meaning of the Old South in history, they have often noted the many ironies in the story. The planters were among the loudest advocates of freedom and equality, yet they rarely found any contradiction between those ideals and the ownership of other humans. They understood the necessity of keeping their slaves under the tightest of coercive controls, yet they often formed close human relationships with those bondsmen. The planter class frequently praised the superiority of the South's rural, agrarian, traditional society over that of the urban, industrializing, and modernizing North, yet most of the planters were practical-minded businessmen who ran their plantations with an eye toward efficiency and profitability. They almost always had claimed to be patriotic, Union-loving Americans, yet as a class they overwhelmingly supported southern independence in 1861.

Kenneth Rayner of North Carolina embodied all of these contradictions, and more. Born into a slaveholding family of modest means in the Albemarle Sound region in 1808, he studied law and won a seat in the lower house of the North Carolina legislature in 1835. As a young lawmaker, he cast his lot with the Whig Party and in 1839 was elected to Congress, where he supported Whig programs such as tariffs, state aid to transportation, and a national banking system. Despite being a large-scale planter and slaveholder, he would also become a strong unionist and opponent of proslavery sectionalism.

Kenneth Rayner's intelligence, rugged good looks, and dazzling ability as an orator caught the eye of a Raleigh belle named Susan Polk, the youngest daughter of the late Col. William Polk, one of the richest men in the state. When the couple married in 1842, Susan brought to the marriage an inheritance of some 20,000 acres in North Carolina and Tennessee. Along with Susan's bank and railroad stock, an indeterminate number of slaves, and the small plantation that he had inherited from his own father, Rayner now controlled an estate worth more than $100,000. He was poised to move into the first rank of the South's great planters.

Rayner retired from Congress in 1845 to concentrate on his private business affairs. Returning with Susan to Raleigh, the couple moved into the Polk family mansion that Susan had inherited upon her mothers death. Over the next few years Rayner greatly expanded his holdings in land and slaves, including the purchase of a large plantation on the Mississippi River in Chicot County, Arkansas. He re-entered the North Carolina legislature, but in the early 1850s he became increasingly dissatisfied with the direction that his beloved Whig Party was taking. Deeply devoted to the Union, Rayner became convinced that both of the old political parties—Whigs and Democrats alike—were succumbing to the pressures of sectionalism. He particularly despised the Democratic Party, convinced that it was using the votes of recently naturalized immigrants in the North to maintain a corrupt alliance with secessionists in the South. In 1854 Rayner helped to found the American Party (called the Know-Nothings by its critics), which was dedicated to slowing the flood of European emigrants pouring into the country and diminishing the political influence of old-stock Americans. He soon emerged as one of the party's leading national figures. The Know-Nothings offered a unionist alternative to the increasingly proslavery Democrats, the soon-to-disappear Whigs, and the new antislavery Republicans. When the

American Party, like the Whigs, finally collapsed under the pressures of sectionalism, Rayner found himself a man without a party. In April 1861 he traveled to Arkansas to oversee planting operations on his plantation there. As the steamboat approached his river landing to pick him up for the return trip home, he heard the ship's captain cry out that Fort Sumter had fallen. "Yes," Rayner remarked to a companion standing beside him, "and I fear the South has fallen with it."

Kenneth Rayner's attitudes toward slavery and sectionalism set him apart from the majority of American slaveholders in the years leading up to the Civil War. Despite the fact that he owned more than 200 slaves by 1860, he never claimed—as did many slaveholders and southern politicians—that slavery was a positive good. Indeed, he clung to the older, Jeffersonian description of slavery as a necessary evil. Thomas Jefferson thought that virtue and intelligence were the prerequisites to citizenship in a republic, and that slaves—not because of their inherent racial inferiority but because of their degraded social position—lacked those essential qualities. "I do not say that [slavery] is the best conditions they [blacks] are capable of," Rayner once wrote. "In the dispensation of Providence they may reach a higher standard of civilization in some other position." Few slaveholders in the 1850s were willing to concede such a possibility.

Rayner took pride in being a paternalistic slaveowner. He claimed that his North Carolina slaves "lived in better houses than a majority of the poor white people in the country—frame tenements, plastered and whitewashed, with every fixture and convenience necessary for comfort." When he purchased his Arkansas plantation, he made careful inquiries into the "humanity and attention to comfort, observed towards slaves" in the neighborhood. According to Rayner's own testimony, his neighbors remarked that "they had never witnessed so strong an attachment between owners and slaves as existed between my family and our slaves. I know the fact that it was the common boast of my slaves that they had the best master in the world." Commenting on his family's slaves, Rayner believed that he "never saw a more joyous, happy and contented set of beings."

As with most slaveholders, there must have been a large measure of self-delusion in his assertions. Whatever modest material comforts his slaves may have enjoyed, rare was the slave who would not have traded these for freedom. Moreover, in the case of Kenneth Rayner, there was more to the master-slave relationship than he boasted. On November 13, 1850, a fifteen-year-old Rayner family slave named Mary Ricks—herself a mulatto—gave birth to a son whose father was obviously white. Whether Mary was raped outright or simply surrendered to her master's overtures makes little difference; given the power relationship (not to mention the age difference) between the two, the liaison was necessarily exploitative. The black descendants of Kenneth Rayner agree that Rayner made no effort to conceal the parternity of this child and his two other mulatto children. But it should not surprise us that he either tacitly or openly acknowledged his mulatto offspring and afforded them special treatment. Given Kenneth Rayner's temperament and the prevailing notions of honor and propriety in North Carolina elite society, it would be surprising had he done otherwise.

Historians who have examined the dynamics of miscegenation (race mixing) in the Old South have shed much light on the nature of master-slave sexual liaisons. Surprisingly, southern society did not always openly condemn the unions between male slaveholders and their female slaves. The leading historian of the southern moral code has explained that such relationships posed almost no ethical problems for the antebellum southern community, so long as the rules, which were fairly easy to follow, were discreetly observed. Those rules dictated that the union be "a casual one in which the disparity of rank and race between the partners was quite clear to any observer" and that "the pairing could not be part of a general pattern of dissoluteness." According to this scholar, "a man should by all means never acknowledge in mixed company his illicit liaison with a woman, black *or* white." Scandal, according to another historian, "was perhaps worse than the deed itself."

Mary Chestnut, an aristocratic southern woman whose life had much in common with that of Susan Rayner, wrote an analysis that easily could have described the Rayner household. "Like the patriarchs of old," wrote Chesnut in 1861, "our men live all in one house with their wives and their concubines, and the mulattoes one sees in every family exactly resemble the white children—and every lady tells you who is the father of all the mulatto children in everybody's household, but those in her own she seems to think drop from the clouds, or pretends so to think." It comes as no surprise, then, that Kenneth Rayner's illicit affair with Mary Ricks attracted little attention during his lifetime. He probably did not discuss this union, his white family certainly did not, and political opponents in North Carolina never would have broached the subject. To criticize a wealthy southern planter-politician on such grounds nearly always would have backfired, so common was the vice among Rayner's contemporaries. As one former North Carolina slave recalled, "At dat time it wus a hard job to find a marster dat didn't have women 'mong his slaves. Dat wus a generel thing 'mong the slave owners."

Mary Ricks' child, named John Baptis Rayner, was probably born on his father's farm on the outskirts of Raleigh. As an adult he would generally sign his name using only the initials "J. B." instead of "John"—a common practice among men of that era. Either at birth or in early childhood, the boy was taken from his mother and brought to the mansion in town, where he was placed in the care of his maternal great-grandfather, Henry Jett, who raised him. Jett was born a slave, but he had been freed by the provisions of Col. William Polk's will. He had spent his life in the service of the Polk and Rayner families. Although his ostensible job was that of carriage driver, Jett appears to have fulfilled the dual roles of manager and patriarch of the Polk-Rayner slaves in Raleigh. There were reasons, however, for Jett's privileged status.

Henry Jett's parentage cannot be stated with absolute certainty, but his black descendants agree that he was blood kin to the Polks. In all probability, he was the illegitimate son of Revolutionary War general Thomas Polk, Susan Rayner's grandfather. Speculation as to his mother's identity has ranged from that of a mulatto slave woman to an Italian mistress of Thomas Polk. Whatever his parentage, Jett did not possess much "Negro blood," for his photograph gives every appearance of a white man. With Thomas Polk's death, the family slaves passed to his son. Susan Rayner's father, Col. William Polk, thus found himself in the strange position—not so terribly uncommon in the Old South—of owning his own half-brother. Jett married another Polk slave, Matilda, who bore him a large family, and he lived to see his granddaughter Mary give birth to John Rayner. By this time the Polk family mansion in Raleigh and the offspring of Henry and Matilda Jett had become the property of Kenneth and Susan Rayner as part of Susan's inheritance. Since Henry Jett's wife and their large family were still slaves, Jett continued to live in the servants' quarters and work for Kenneth Rayner, even though he was technically a free man. Two female mulatto children of Kenneth Rayner (John's half-sisters) were similarly placed in the care of Henry and Matilda.

Oral tradition among John Rayner's descendants holds that the boy John was brought into the Kenneth Rayner household without much regard for the sentiments of Susan or the other white family members. Whatever Susan thought initially, she, like so many southern women, had no choice but to accommodate Kenneth's mulatto children. It was no more than her own grandmother had done fifty years earlier when she had been forced to tolerate the special treatment accorded to Henry Jett by Thomas Polk. During the Know-Nothing campaigns of the mid-1850s, Kenneth spent many weeks away from home, and Susan would have had to play her part in the management of the Raleigh household, with its large contingent of white and black members. Even after the decline of Know-Nothingism, Kenneth spent much time visiting his far-flung planting empire. With her husband gone so much, Susan's contacts with her husband's illegitimate children must have been frequent and not altogether pleasant. They were, after all, not only Kenneth's offspring but her own blood relatives. During the war, Susan managed the Confederate soldiers' hospital in Raleigh. John's half-sister Cornelia told her descendants about Susan Rayner taking the mulatto children with her to the hospital to assist in the care of wounded soldiers. In addition, the Rayners opened their home to a number of wounded Confederate officers, and in later years John Rayner recalled helping to care for them.

Despite his long record as a unionist, Kenneth Rayner served in North Carolina's secession convention, and after Lincoln's call for troops he supported southern independence. Rayner's duties in the secession convention and the location of his plantations near the theaters of war caused him to reside primarily in Raleigh through the years of his John's early adolescence. It was a fascinating environment for a boy of that age. John Rayner could not have avoided hearing some of the public speeches that his father made in the 1850s and 1860s, and his own oratorical style would later bear the unmistakable imprint of this exposure. Even for a slave boy, reaching adolescence in the Kenneth Rayner household a few blocks away from the state capitol must have provided unusual opportunities to observe politics. Especially during the secession crisis and the early phases of the Civil War, the Rayner mansion was the scene of a nearly constant parade of important political figures. North Carolina Chief Justice Thomas Ruffin, Kenneth Rayner's law mentor, spent many nights under his friend's roof, and very few days passed without the Rayners inviting a visiting legislator, former governor, or Confederate officer into their cordial home. Exactly what influence this environment had on John Rayner, who would have been scarcely seen and never heard, is difficult to say. But it could not have been negligible.

In his later years, the younger Rayner vividly remembered the surrender of Raleigh. Writing in 1904, he recalled helping the family hide "cotton and other valuables" from the rapidly advancing Union army. He also related the story of a young Confederate soldier who fired at Sherman's advance troops as they entered Raleigh in 1865. Federal authorities quickly apprehended the renegade and after a quick trial sentenced him to hang. "In carrying him to the place of execution," John Rayner recollected, "they had to pass in front of Judge Rayner's mansion, and my boyish curiosity caused me to follow them." John claimed to have pleaded with the authorities for the condemned man's life when he realized that the soldier was to be hanged.

John may have received the rudiments of an education even before emancipation. Urban slaves of aristocratic masters enjoyed vastly greater opportunities for education than their counterparts from the cotton fields. Henry Jett probably was literate, for he was chosen in 1868 to lead a secession of 200 black members from Raleigh's previously racially mixed First Baptist Church, founding the First Colored Baptist Church. If John was not taught to read and write prior to emancipation, he at least was given religious training, for Jett was described at the time of his death as "a consistent member of the church" for more than sixty years. However, it was only after the fall of the Confederacy that John Rayner's education really began.

Kenneth Rayner's outlook toward the newly freed slaves shifted in the immediate aftermath of the war. Initially he despaired of blacks being able to function as productive free laborers, and he knew that southern whites would refuse to recognize them as fellow citizens. Thus he, like many other upper-class whites in the South and the North, advocated the colonization of the newly freed people to Africa as the only practicable solution. Throughout the course of 1866, however, Rayner's attitudes changed. He realized that blacks and whites were both in the South to stay, and he revised his initial predictions. He came to believe that, with the proper guidance of whites, the freedmen might be able to adjust to their freedom and become productive citizens much more quickly than he had first thought.

One episode during 1866 helped Rayner make this transition. On one of his postwar trips to the Northeast, the North Carolinian paid a visit to his old friend Gen. O. O. Howard, who as head of the Freedmen's Bureau was then deeply involved in the federal government's early experiments in African American education. Howard recalled in his autobiography that Rayner, whom the former Union general "had long known and valued as a personal friend, came to my room to labor with me and show me how unwise were some of my ideas." Howard recalled Rayner's initial skepticism about educating blacks. "General Howard," Rayner supposedly said, "do you not know that you are educating the colored youth above their business? You will only destroy them. Those young girls, for example; they will be too proud or vain to work, and the consequence will be that they will go to dance houses and other places of improper resort." Howard was "astonished" that Rayner expressed such an opinion, and the general set out to prove his friend mistaken.

Howard took Rayner across the street from his headquarters to the "seminary" in which black teenage girls were being taught. First they visited a music class and heard one girl sing while another accompanied her on the organ. As Howard looked on approvingly, Rayner's "eyes moistened" and he whispered, "They always could sing!" Next the two men sat in on a reading class, where the ability of the students and good order of the classroom made a deep impression on Rayner. Howard wrote that his friend "had seldom seen" such an impressive school, "even of whites." As the former slaveholder and Union general left the school and walked back across the street arm in arm, Rayner told Howard, "General, you have converted me!" Before leaving, Rayner promised to lend his support to efforts for black education at home.

Kenneth Rayner had always believed that *environment* played a large part in determining human potential, in contrast with the more popular competing theories that posited the natural inferiority of non–Anglo Americans. As a Know-Nothing, he had maintained that immigrants needed twenty-one years of "training" in the ways of Americanism before being granted U.S. citizenship and the right to vote; it comes as no surprise, then, that he entertained certain reservations about the integration of blacks into American society. His rejection of biological determinism, however, revealed that Rayner's opinions on blacks' potential could be shaped and revised as new evidence demonstrated that they could indeed learn quickly.

Despite considerable opposition from many native whites, a number of schools for the freedmen were established in Raleigh in the first years after the war. In 1866 or 1867 young John Rayner enrolled in the Raleigh Theological Institute, later renamed Shaw University. Founded in 1866 by a New England Baptist minister and receiving support from the Freedmen's Bureau, the New England Freedmen's Aid Society, and the American Baptist Home Mission Society, the school's primary mission was to train black ministers.

As the Raleigh Theological Institute was making its first efforts to educate the former slaves, a group of prominent North Carolina Episcopalians were founding yet another educational institution, St. Augustine's Normal and Collegiate Institute. Incorporated in July 1867 under the auspices of the Episcopal Church to train black schoolteachers and ministers, St. Augustine's incorporators included several of Kenneth Rayner's personal friends. The school opened its doors to students in January 1868 on land adjoining Kenneth Rayner's property in Raleigh, and at some point John B. Rayner enrolled in the new school. St. Augustine's was the institution that Kenneth Rayner had promised Gen. O. O. Howard he would help promote, and John Rayner's descendants recalled that Kenneth donated money to the school. Although the surviving records are not entirely clear, it seems that the elder Rayner rented the Raleigh mansion to Dr. J. Brinton Smith, first principal of the school. During St. Augustine's first term, some of the female students roomed in the house, while the male students lived in the adjoining servants' quarters. It appears, then, that in the case of John Rayner, the usual practice whereby students leave home for college was reversed—the college came to him.

Kenneth Rayner could rent his home to the new freedmen's school because he had decided to leave North Carolina for good. Rayner wanted to be closer to his cotton plantations on the Mississippi River, the means by which he hoped to recover his fortune, which the war had badly wrecked. In June 1867 he, Susan, and their children departed for Memphis, taking a few of their ex-slaves with them. Seventeen-year-old John and his two mulatto half-sisters, however, stayed in Raleigh. After Kenneth's departure from North Carolina, there is no surviving record of communication between him and John, although John monitored his father's subsequent political career. They may have kept in touch, perhaps discussing politics and exchanging news about the white and black branches of the family, but it seems unlikely. In the numerous personal letters of Kenneth Rayner that have survived from the Civil War period, he never specifically mentioned his mulatto children, and in 1866 he wrote that "none of us have any ties to sever" in leaving Raleigh. Kenneth Rayner in 1867 wished to leave behind the life that the war had irrevocably shattered. But ever-paternalistic toward his former slaves, for whom he apparently had sincere affection, Kenneth saw to it that his son John received what advantages an education could bring. Having fulfilled what he perceived as his responsibility to the young man, the father then turned his back on the son. Such was the legacy of slavery and racism in the South; blacks and whites found their lives undeniably interconnected, yet worlds apart.

John pursued his education until about 1870, at which time the census listed both him and one sister as living in the household of Edward Lane, a thirty-year-old mulatto carriage driver who resided in a predominantly black neighborhood. The census taker did not record an occupation for John, so it is likely that he was still a student, renting a room from the Lanes. At St. Augustine's Rayner received an education of surprising thoroughness. The curriculum in the mid-1870s included the basics of English, history, and mathematics, although it placed heavy emphasis on Greek and Latin classical literature—including the works of Homer, Plato, Herodotus, Thucydides, Virgil, and Cicero. This formal classical education would be reflected throughout John Rayner's life in his writings and speeches.

Although he had not graduated, sometime between June 1870 and November 1872 John Rayner ended his education and left Raleigh. He taught briefly in rural schools near Raleigh, but teaching did not completely satisfy his ambitions. Now Rayner's destination was Tarboro, in Edgecombe County, two counties east of Raleigh. Tarboro was the same town in which, nearly fifty years earlier, his father had attended the academy and begun studying law. John had just turned twenty-one, and a young, educated, black North Carolinian interested in politics could have found no better place to embark upon an exciting political career.

Located in the heart of the most heavily black section of the state, Edgecombe County in 1870 had a population of nearly 23,000, two-thirds of whom were African Americans. When the Reconstruction Acts of 1867 enfranchised blacks, the Republican Party easily gained control of the county's politics and soon established a strong biracial political coalition that moved swiftly and confidently toward securing equal rights for all citizens. As elsewhere in the South, blacks held a minority of the elective offices, but black voters placed in positions of power white Republicans who were expected to represent black interests. Those blacks who did attain elective positions most commonly filled the lower-level local and county offices, which nonetheless provided valuable grassroots training for the first generation of southern black political leadership. John Rayner, as a young, articulate, educated African American who grew up in the eye of the political hurricane in North Carolina, naturally was attracted to such an environment.

His upbringing and education were not the only ways in which Rayner defied white stereotypes of "Negroes." Both blacks and whites often commented on his physical appearance, for Rayner was so light-skinned that he could almost "pass" for white. Relatively short in stature, but built like a bull, his broad nose and wavy hair suggested his African ancestry more than did his parchment-colored complexion. In the North he might easily have posed as an immigrant of Mediterranean origins. He spoke in a surprisingly high but clear voice, with an accent more resembling that of an upper-class white southerner than that of most blacks, although he certainly knew the common black vernacular and could employ it on the political stump when useful.

John Rayner would sometimes be described as a "white nigger" by whites and viewed with suspicion by some blacks. His mostly Caucasian genetic inheritance, his upbringing in the Kenneth Rayner household, and his polished education and manners placed him in a paradoxical situation. He was acutely aware that the only thing preventing him from enjoying life as a full-fledged member of the South's ruling class was the accident of having been born to a slave mother. Intellectually he was the equal of any white man. His oratorical ability was unsurpassed by any white politician of his day. He enjoyed hobnobbing with white political allies, to whom he sometimes joked about the minuscule amount of "Negro blood" in his veins. His attitudes toward the black masses were at best paternalistic—and at worst condescending—when he boasted to white associates about knowing the "eccentricities" of blacks.

One suspects that deep down John Rayner never really considered himself a "Negro." But he accepted the reality of his situation and, in a surprising sort of way, even embraced it. It is clear that he harbored an intense affection and sympathy for the downtrodden black people of the South, even as he frequently criticized them for what he perceived as their shortcomings. No matter how illogical or unfair it might sometimes have seemed to him, African Americans were his "people." He could have done what both of his mulatto half-sisters did—leave the South, move to New York, and frequently pass as white—but there is no record that he ever considered leaving the South or tried to avoid being considered a "Negro" by whites.

However small his actual African genetic inheritance, Rayner lived all his life in a South that still adhered scrupulously to the "one-drop rule"; that is to say, one drop of "Negro blood" made one a "Negro." And during Reconstruction, no place could have better epitomized the Deep South, with all its racial phobias, than Tarboro, North Carolina. It was like a setting from a William Faulkner novel—a place of honor with sensitive, aristocratic planters, struggling poor white dirt farmers, masses of oppressed freedmen, and herds of pigs rooting about the dusty streets. By night the Union League (a secret, pro-Republican, and problack political organization) and its opposite number, the Ku Klux Klan, secretly organized. Blacks and the lower classes of whites mingled along the Tar River waterfront in a district of saloons and brothels known tellingly as "Grab All." The unreconstructed editor of the town's Democratic newspaper, the *Tarboro Southerner,* proudly quoted Jefferson Davis on the masthead of his paper: "I AM A SOUTHERN MAN, OF SOUTHERN PRINCIPLES." The local sheriff jailed the editor twice in four years to keep him out of duels.

The surviving historical record provides only a meager outline of John Rayner's life and activities during his years in Tarboro. In keeping with the rough-and-tumble character of the town, he appears to have sown a few wild oats as a young bachelor. In November 1872 he was summoned by the Edgecombe Superior Court to testify in a bastardy case. The mother, one Eliza Lawrence, claimed that Rayner had fathered her illegitimate child, a charge that he did not deny. The court ordered him to pay court costs and post a bastardy bond to compensate the county in the event that the child became a public burden. The following spring Rayner again ran afoul of the law and was found guilty of assault and battery. Neither of these episodes was serious enough to warrant explanation in the local press, but they suggest that he was something less than the pious man that his collegiate theology instructors had trained him to be. Such indiscretions apparently did little to prevent Rayner's entry into politics, for in 1873 he was appointed to the first of a number of local political offices.

The following year Rayner married a fair-skinned mulatto woman named Susan Staten. Performing the ceremony was Tarboro's white Episcopal priest, Joseph Blount Cheshire, a family friend of the Kenneth Rayner's who had been one of the founders of St. Augustine's University. Clearly John had not severed all ties to North Carolinas white elites or to his own past. The newlyweds settled down to the business of making a living and starting a family. Little is known about the nature of their marital relationship, but two years later the union produced a daughter, Mary.

John Rayner entered Edgecombe County Republican politics with his appointment as constable of the grand jury for the fall 1873 session of the Superior Court. He held this position intermittently for the next five years, serving again in fall of 1874, spring and summer of 1876, and spring of 1878. Edgecombe County during Reconstruction was divided into fourteen townships, each of which elected justices of the peace, school committeemen, and a constable. During the mid-1870s a small coterie of black and white Republicans shared these offices, with individuals often holding these county offices concurrently with state or federal positions. The voters of Tarboro Township elected Rayner justice of the peace in August 1875 by a straight party vote, and he served in that capacity until his term expired in 1877. Under the state's Reconstruction constitution, justices of the peace, also known as magistrates, enjoyed considerable power. They presided in civil suits involving amounts of $200 or less and in criminal cases punishable by a maximum of one month in jail or a $50 fine. In addition, two magistrates plus a clerk in each township constituted a Board of Trustees which, under the supervision of the county commissioners, assessed taxes, administered elections, and maintained roads and bridges. As magistrate and trustee, Rayner received invaluable experience in grassroots politics.

Despite Rayner's and other blacks' success in Edgecombe County politics, the area was no utopia for African Americans during Reconstruction. If he had not experienced it already, Rayner's first years in politics gave him firsthand exposure to white supremacy in some of its most virulent forms. The county's population was so heavily black that no amount of effort on the part of white Democrats—short of the legal disfranchisement of blacks—was ever going to put an end to black political participation. This reality, bleak as it was to prejudiced whites, did little to encourage a spirit of acceptance or reconciliation among the Democrats. Fierce racial animosities in Tarboro never subsided during Rayner's years there. In 1872 the editor of the *Tarboro Southerner*, William Biggs, echoed the sentiments of the county's unreconstructed white populace when he wrote that "the negro, with some exceptions, in his present state, is depraved, ignorant, brutal, and filled with all the evil depravities to which human nature is subject." Cataloging the many alleged transgressions of the freedmen, including the standard charge that black men had "defiled the chastity and outraged the virtue of thousands of Southern women," the Democratic editor openly defended lynching. Not surprisingly, Biggs's outspokenness nearly got him killed when he attended a Republican rally and, in his own words, "was fallen upon by a mob of negro and white assassins." Fortunately for the editor, two black men came to his rescue. Such was the political environment that John Rayner had entered.

The Republican grip on the county showed no signs of weakening as Rayner became more deeply involved in local politics, although Democrats went to extraordinary lengths to keep Republicans out of office. These included a campaign mounted in 1874 to prevent the Republicans from posting the cash bonds that public officials were required to post to insure the county against embezzlement. The types of rhetoric used in the anti–bond-signing campaign would become the stock-in-trade of Democratic politicians for the next fifty years. The *Southerner* fired the first shots in the campaign with the challenge, *"If there is a southern man of southern principles in Edgecombe county who desires Social Equality, . . . Mixed Schools, . . . [and] intermarriage between the races, let him put his signature to* [a Republicans] *bond!!!"*

Such demagoguery proved fruitless in Tarboro during Rayner's time there. Enough financially secure Tarboro citizens were willing to commit "treason to party and race" to enable white and black

Republicans to post bond and take office. The working relationship between blacks such as Rayner and white Radicals (Republicans) such as Sheriff Joseph Cobb proved remarkably durable. In fact, Cobb's and Rayner's association extended to private business dealings, with the white sheriff on one occasion loaning the black magistrate $250. But the Democrats never gave up. When Republicans again were required to post bonds in 1875, the Democratic press again called on all whites to refuse to sign. Not only were black officeholders a slap in the face of white supremacy, they alleged, but magistrates like Rayner, whom Democrats claimed were "hardly . . . able to read and write," were making a "farce" out of county government. "Oh God!" cried the *Southerner,* "think of the insult you offer your children when you put your signature to the bonds of such men." The campaign again failed, and Rayner won election and posted bond.

The cries of "social equality," "mixed schools," and "intermarriage between the races" proved, in time, to be powerful rhetoric in the hands of southern Democrats. In reality, neither Radical Republicans in the 1870s nor Populists in the 1890s ever seriously advocated full legal equality for African Americans, which would become the mark of racial liberalism in the mid-twentieth century. What the Democrats in Tarboro were really seeking was not to prevent some imagined "social equality" but rather to defeat the Republicans by ostracizing anyone who supported them. By Democratic standards, guaranteeing a Republican's bond branded one a traitor to white supremacy.

The ambitious young politician had achieved his first elective office, but over the next two years, things went sour for Rayner in Tarboro. The large Democratic majority elected to the state legislature in 1874 passed a bill calling for a convention to revise the 1868 state constitution. After debating frivolous questions such as who was the "original carpetbagger"—Jesus Christ or Judas Iscariot—the 1875 convention eventually passed thirty amendments, one of which took the right to elect magistrates away from the voters and gave it to the state legislature. North Carolina (in the terminology of the triumphant Democrats, who wished to restore prewar race relations in the South and tear down many of Reconstruction's institutions) had been "redeemed." As the Tarboro Southerner explained, "we consented to give up our much-loved right of electing Magistrates by the people, so that the incompetent carpetbaggers and negroes would have to stand aside." After his term expired in 1877, Rayner was no longer justice of the peace.

The year 1877 was eventful for Rayner in several other respects. Not only did his tenure as magistrate end, but his private business interests suffered. In 1875 Rayner had entered into a business partnership with local political figure John W. Gant, whom the *Southerner* described as "a white Republican of the blackest description." The two partners in the firm of Gant & Rayner bought a lot fronting the Tar River, adjacent to the saloon-and-brothel district Grab All, and the county commissioners were granted them a retail liquor license. The precise nature of the business of Gant & Rayner cannot be known; it probably was not a brothel, given the proprietors' status as local political leaders. More likely, Rayner and his partner were running a saloon, restaurant, or general store, any of which might have occasion to apply for a liquor license.

Most of Grab All was situated on land owned by the city of Tarboro and leased to assorted businesses. Gant and Rayner owned their property, but it adjoined the portion of Grab All owned by the city. In 1877 the leases of the city's tenants expired, and the county commissioners decided to clean up these dens of iniquity. The government moved swiftly, not only evicting their tenants but demolishing the "various tenements defacing the spot." After the commissioners acted, the *Southerner* reported that "Grab All is as silent as some 'banquet hall deserted, whose lights are fled, whose whiskeys dead, and all but the scent departed.' Gant is gone, The others forlorn. Gone to mourn over past glories." While their privately owned building presumably escaped demolition, Gant & Rayner was a casualty of the county's moral crusade.

The nearly simultaneous end of his term as magistrate and demise of his private business brought Rayner to a crossroads in his life. Three months after the destruction of Grab All, a black Baptist evangelist from Washington, D.C., came to Tarboro and held a series of revival meetings. On the fourth Sunday of May he baptized thirty-eight black men and women in the Tar River. Rayner was among them, and he became a member of the Colored Missionary Baptist Church. Despite his great-grandfather Henry Jett's role in the founding of Raleigh's First Colored Baptist Church, Rayner in his early life apparently had followed the example of his white relatives and been confirmed as an Episcopalian. He had been trained in Episcopalian theology at St. Augustine's, and he had been married in the Episcopal Church. Nevertheless, Rayner's baptism into a new faith also opened the door to a new career, even as his political career seemed to be drawing to a close. He was ordained to preach, adding the vocation of Baptist minister to his prior occupations of teacher, politician, and merchant. Three months later Rayner sold his interest in the Grab All property. Before long, North Carolina would belong to his past.

Although stripped of his magistrate's office, Rayner served one more appointed term as constable of the superior court in 1878. Edgecombe County and the Second Congressional District of which it was a part continued to elect black legislators and congressmen, but many of the local positions that had traditionally served as springboards to higher offices now were reserved for whites. Perhaps Rayner had not advanced far enough up the political ladder to ever stand a chance of election to a higher post, or maybe financial considerations persuaded him to seek a change. It is also possible that his conversion to the Baptist Church and the call to preach led him to consider relocating to a region where educated black clergy were in high demand. Most likely, some combination of these factors was at work when Rayner decided to seek a new home—in Texas.

Rayner was not alone in choosing to leave North Carolina in 1879–1880. Conditions for the vast majority of blacks, who toiled as tenant farmers or sharecroppers, had deteriorated steadily through the 1870s. The Redeemer legislature of 1876–1877 quickly conjured up a draconian Landlord and Tenant Act that took away virtually all rights of tenant farmers, including a clause making violation of tenancy agreements a criminal offense. With such a law on the books and only predominantly Democratic courts to enforce it, black farmers found themselves hopelessly bound to the land and indebted to white landlords. If the Redeemers had wished to effect a return to the Old South, they had largely succeeded, but their plan was to backfire.

In 1879 blacks began to leave North Carolina and other southern states in substantial numbers. Not only had the harsh Landlord and Tenant Act restricted blacks' rights and opportunities, but the loss of the right to elect magistrates, the denial of blacks' right to sit on juries, and the end of black control over their public schools rankled the freedmen. Radical Reconstruction had sought permanently to secure these fundamental rights for blacks but had failed. Now Rayner and thousands of other African Americans who had experienced the empty promise of Reconstruction were to spend the next twenty-five years attempting to regain what they had so quickly lost under Redemption. By late 1879 the exodus from North Carolina had reached such proportions that white planters, fearing the wholesale loss of their inexpensive black labor force, became truly alarmed. While many blacks emigrated to Indiana and other Midwest destinations, some of the so-called exodusters landed in the Southwest, including Texas. Meanwhile, the flow of blacks from North Carolina attracted national attention and finally resulted in a congressional investigation.

Rayner's own search for a fresh start coincided with the mounting exodus. In about 1879 Horatio "Rasche" Hearne, a wealthy planter from Robertson County, Texas, traveled to North Carolina with one of his plantation managers in an effort to recruit black laborers. With North Carolina planters working diligently to halt the emigration, men like Hearne would have to find local intermediaries if they hoped to recruit black workers successfully. While the evidence is largely circumstantial, it is almost certain that Hearne hired Rayner to serve as one such intermediary. As a well-connected local leader who could speak the language of both blacks and whites, Rayner was the perfect choice. His education and legal experience as a former justice of the peace enabled him to see that those he recruited were being offered a fair deal, and perhaps most important, he was prepared to move to Texas with them. A number of Hearne's fellow Robertson County planters helped fund his enterprise, and they secured laborers from North Carolina "in proportion to the

contributions they had made toward the expenses of the project."
Ultimately Hearne recruited "several trainloads" of blacks from North
Carolina. As one of the county's white old-timers reminisced decades
later, "For many years, when a Robertson County Negro was asked
if he had been born in Texas, he would answer, 'No sir, Mr. Hearne
fotch [sic] me out here from North Carolina.'" Oral tradition among
his descendants places the number of exodusters Rayner led to Texas
at perhaps one thousand.

When the federal census was taken in 1880, Rayner already had
arrived in the town of Calvert, Robertson County. While it is possible that the final arrangements for the emigrants may have prompted
one or more trips to and from Tarboro to Calvert, to the best knowledge of Rayner's descendants, he never returned to North Carolina
after 1880. Rayner's situation likely resembled that which the *New
York Times* described in an October 1879 editorial on the North
Carolina exodus: "The negroes who have been sent out to prepare
the way before the intending emigrants are notified from home that
it would be unsafe for them to return, so violent are the threats made
against them by their former masters and present employers." Whether
or not Rayner was in Texas to stay in June 1880, by May of the next
year he and his family had definitely settled into their new home, a
comfortable frame house in the black section of Calvert purchased
with the money Rayner had earned for his recruiting efforts.

As the black exodus from North Carolina reached its peak in
late 1879, the *New York Times* observed that the condition of the
black farmers (in North Carolina) differed "from the old bondage in
little beyond the name." White lawmakers and landowners were attempting "to reconcile the nearest possible approach to slavery with
the nominal continuance of freedom." Having experienced the promise and the failure of Reconstruction as a grassroots leader, John B.
Rayner could testify to the truth of such a statement. Radical Reconstruction, with its brave experiment in biracial politics, had resulted
in little more than shattered expectations and new forms of oppression for those who had embraced its challenge to the South's old
order. Rayner was discovering firsthand the limits that the white South
placed on black political participation. But at age thirty he was hardly
prepared to resign himself to a fatalistic acceptance of those limits.

# CHAPTER TWO

# The Search for a Political Voice

JOHN B. RAYNER'S new home in Texas shared much in common
with his old one in North Carolina. With 49 percent of the population made up of ex-slaves and their families, Robertson County was
heavily black by Texas standards. The county ranked in the top ten
cotton-producing counties in the state. Calvert, located in the western part of the county at the edge of the rich alluvial Brazos River
bottom, was the largest town in the county, with a population of
2,280. Proceeding north and east from Calvert, one moves into a
brushier region of gently rolling hills interrupted by small rivers and
creeks. Cotton grew best in the river and creek bottoms, but the soil
throughout the county was reasonably good, and farmers outside
the bottoms raised a variety of crops, including cotton. The African
American population, however, resided heavily in the southern and
western sections of the county, where the large planters grew cotton
on a grand scale.

Rayner's new home also resembled his old one in its recent political history. When the Civil War ended, Robertson County planters, who had ardently supported the Confederate war effort, experienced, in their words, the "heavy burden" of Reconstruction. Union
troops briefly occupied the county, the Freedmen's Bureau established
a station in it, and following the passage of the 1867 Reconstruction
Acts, African Americans played an important role in county govern-

ment. In fact, well into the 1890s—long after the end of Reconstruction—the heavily black precincts, including the towns of Calvert and Hearne, continued to elect black county commissioners, constables, sheriffs, and four different state representatives. The high degree of opposition to the Democratic Party and the active participation of blacks in that opposition set the county apart from most others in the South. Indeed, it probably had a strong bearing on Rayner's decision to settle there. Moreover, beginning in the 1870s and continuing through the 1890s, Robertson County was a hotbed of third-party activity. Rayner became involved in these political movements and eventually came to lead the most important of them.

When Rayner came to Calvert in 1880, the state was in the midst of the second Greenback campaign. The Greenback Party was an agrarian third-party movement devoted to increasing the amount of money in circulation, causing inflation, and thereby easing the hard times that debt-strapped farmers faced. (Debtors benefit from inflation because they can repay their debts in depreciated currency.) Although founded and led by whites, the Greenback movement in Robertson County had been heavily black and had even gained the support of the county Republican organization against their common enemy, the Democrats. Two African American Greenbackers from the county won seats in the state legislature in 1878 and 1880, and Calvert's own William H. Hamman, an ex-Confederate general, won the Greenback nomination for governor, evidence of the effectiveness of the local black-white coalition. But such biracial coalitions were always fragile in the post–Reconstruction South, for they usually lacked the support of party organizations at the state and national levels. Furthermore, white Greenbackers as well as black Republicans often balked at the prospect of interracial cooperation. Nevertheless, the tradition of biracial political activism was already strong in Robertson County when Rayner arrived there in 1880—a factor crucial in understanding his subsequent career.

Rayner maintained a low political profile during his early years in Calvert, concentrating on making a living by teaching school and perhaps occasionally preaching. His family responsibilities grew, for in November 1882 Susan gave birth to their second child, a boy named

Ivan Edward. Rayner apparently displayed little interest in again running for an elective position, even though African Americans continued to win local offices in the county. He was, after all, a newcomer to a place where established black leaders likely were reluctant to share power. Still, Rayner had not forsaken politics. As time passed, his profile in Calvert's black community grew. He would have been well known among the black farmers in Robertson County's outlying areas because of his role in bringing so many of them from North Carolina. In the small but close-knit black community of Calvert itself, his position as a teacher would have acquainted him with virtually all of the citizenry. And in an environment where poverty and illiteracy were the rule, his exceptional education and proven ability to deal with whites would naturally tend to place him in a position of leadership. As events soon would demonstrate, he was keeping a finger on the political pulse of his adopted community and state. When the chance came to step onto the public stage once more, he would be ready.

Rayner's opportunity came in 1887. Despite their growing division into what were sometimes termed "Bourbon" (conservative) and "agrarian" (progressive) factions, the state Democratic Party had continued successfully to fend off all serious challenges. But in 1887 a new issue threatened Democratic unity: prohibition. Texans had always dealt with the issue of alcohol by means of local option—voters in individual precincts or counties could decide whether to allow the sale of alcoholic beverages. While Democratic politicians well understood that "moral" issues such as prohibition could seriously undermine party unity, by the mid-1880s the small but vocal minority of prohibition activists was proving bothersome, and some even formed their own party to promote their cause. In January 1887 the state executive committee of the Prohibition Party petitioned the state legislature to frame a constitutional amendment banning liquor. Anxious to rid themselves of the issue and confident that voters would reject any such amendment in a statewide referendum, the legislature and the governor agreed to place the measure before the people.

Despite Democratic efforts to portray the prohibition referendum as a nonpartisan issue, it was apparent to Rayner that the election held potentially enormous political ramifications. Prohibition forced politicians to take sides or else give the impression of being weak or unconcerned. Prominent Democrats such as ex-Confederate postmaster general John H. Reagan and U.S. senator Sam Bell Maxey announced their support for the prohibition amendment, as did the majority of the state's Protestant clergymen. At the same time, Gov. Lawrence Sullivan Ross and congressmen Roger Q. Mills, William H. Crain, and James W. Throckmorton actively opposed prohibition, as did state attorney general James S. Hogg, former governor Francis R. Lubbock, and Lt. Gov. Barnett Gibbs. As the campaign heated up in March, the Democrats realized that they had indeed underestimated the divisiveness of the question.

Rayner followed the growing controversy with keen interest. The prohibitionists officially commenced their campaign on March 15. They met in convention at Waco and drafted a plan of organization that included the following resolution: "That we make this campaign as citizens of Texas without reference to race, party politics, religious distinctions or temperance societies as such, leaving to all organizations, moral or religious, to adopt their own methods of helping in this great conflict." At home in Calvert, Rayner realized that the delegates had made a crucial error. While they obviously intended to appeal to black voters, nothing in the prohibitionists' elaborate campaign plan specifically addressed how African American votes were to be won. Yet those votes, if delivered in a bloc, could conceivably make the difference in a closely contested race.

Dr. B. H. Carroll, Texas's most prominent white Baptist minister, chaired the prohibitionist state executive committee. On March 17, two days after the convention, Rayner wrote Carroll a confidential letter pointing out the oversight made in Waco. "Dear Sir," wrote Rayner, "I know that I am not competent to advise you in theology, doctrine, ethics or any of the sciences that have a tendency to make man pure in purpose and angelic in action, but I know something about campaigning and elections." The black politician declared that he was writing because he was "a prohibitionist from deep religious principle." Rayner then reminded Carroll that "the coming campaign will be fought on negroland" and that "the negro vote is quite an item and will play an important part in the coming election." Not being personally acquainted with Carroll, Rayner explained that he had "some little negro in my veins" and he knew "the eccentricities of the negro."

Rayner then laid out his own plan for how the prohibition forces might capture the black vote, bluntly prefacing his outline by telling Carroll something that everybody knew: "money is to be used" in the election by both sides, so the prohibitionists had better know how to put it where it would do the most good. In his first piece of advice, Rayner displayed an attitude that would remain a constant with him for the rest of his life, his distrust and disapproval of traditional African American preachers. "First," he warned, "every old worthless Baptist preacher that has no influence or intellect will seek to be appointed a canvasser in this coming election, and if they fail to get the appointment from the prohibitionists they will offer themselves for sale to the whiskey men." Rayner believed he knew "how to get around this class and still keep them our friends." He proposed "to catch the colored men in three traps": namely, the African Methodist Episcopal Church, the Methodist Episcopal Church, and the Baptist Church. The first step was to have Carroll ask "the bishop of the M.E. church to come to Texas and call a council of his presiding elders in this matter [and state] that he (the bishop) will appoint no preacher to any work next year that will not take a bold stand for the prohibition constitutional amendment, and have the bishop of the African Methodist church to do the same." Rayner named the state's three most influential black Baptist ministers and instructed Carroll to "have these three men to visit all the Baptist associations that are to be held prior to the election and distribute temperance literature and prohibition sermons, etc." He suggested that the "dry," or prohibition, forces give L. G. Jordan, editor of the *Baptist Pilot,* "about $200 for the use of his paper, and have Jordan to send a copy of his paper to every Baptist preacher in this state from now until the election." Jordan had access to a list of all the black Baptist preachers in the state, and Rayner was certain that with this financial inducement Jordan would "strongly defend the amendment from a religious standpoint." "Be sure to look after the colored papers in the state," Rayner added, noting that if Carroll would follow this advice, he would "silence all the old worthless and characterless Baptist preachers that will annoy you and your committee."

Carroll and the prohibition state committee apparently heeded Rayner's suggestions. In the following weeks the prohibitionists began holding rallies throughout the state for African American voters. The black ministers named in Rayner's letter played important roles in these gatherings, and in early June the prohibition press announced the impending arrival of Georgia's Henry M. Turner, bishop of the African Methodist Episcopal Church and one of the most prominent black clergyman in America. Encouraged by the implementation of his plan, Rayner himself began stumping Robertson and the surrounding counties in the service of prohibition.

How did Rayner really feel about prohibition? He told Carroll that his zeal for the cause sprang from "deep religious principle," but this was the same John B. Rayner who had operated a liquor-selling establishment in Tarboro's Grab All district ten years earlier. Perhaps his conversion and baptism into the Baptist faith had wrought a sincere change of heart. But in spite of his professed religious motivations, Rayner embraced prohibition in 1887 not as a minister of the gospel but as a politician. He wanted to play the liquor question for all it was worth, having realized that in prohibition lay the means for seriously injuring the Democratic Party of Texas. From his entry into politics in 1873 until his death forty-five year later, Rayner, like his white father before him, spent the preponderance of his public life in pursuit of one political objective above all others—defeating the Democrats.

The prospects looked bright from the prohibitionist standpoint in the early stages of the campaign, but soon there was trouble. In early June, Rayner's letter to Carroll somehow fell into the hands of the opposition, who quickly made its contents public. The *Vox Populi*, a prohibition paper published in Calvert, charged that the letter had been obtained through "foul means," but there was no proof of the charge. The exposure of the letter was "a devil of a mishap" for the drys, and immediately the "Rayner letter" became a major campaign document for the "wets"(antiprohibitionists). Opponents of prohibition across the state read the letter at antiprohibition rallies. It received widespread attention in the wet press.

The letter badly embarrassed the drys—not because it was bad advice, but indeed because it was such good advice. Here was a way for the wets not only to associate prohibition with blacks but to show the white prohibition leader actually taking advice from a black man. Wet newspapers published Rayner's letter under the headlines "Dark Tactics" and explained that Carroll had "'tumbled' to Bro. Rayner's suggestions." "Rayner is an old and astute politician," jeered the *Calvert Courier,* "and Dr. Carroll is but a new hand at the bellows. They are both Baptist ministers, regularly ordained in the service of Christ, and the proprieties, the Courier believes, are not particularly shocked by the doctor's prompt action upon a masterly suggestion from his colored brother." "Rayner is a shrewd politician," added the *Waco Examiner,* "and understands to a dot how to organize a political campaign. . . ." When seven black clergymen took to the prohibition campaign trail, the wet press dubbed them "Rayner's Seven." By early July, the *Examiner* could say, with considerable accuracy, that "the success of the [antiprohibition] cause has never been doubtful for one moment . . . since Parson Rayner came to Parson Carroll's help with advice as to how to run the campaign. The antis should see to it that Rayner has a nice little monument when he dies."

As it became clear that the contest would be fought on both racial and religious grounds, the campaign assumed a character quite different from its original nonpartisanship. Both sides engaged in demagoguery. A prohibition leader charged that the liquor interests were catering to the "bo-Dutch" [German immigrants] and "buck niggers" in their efforts to keep Texas wet. The antiprohibitionists, in turn, accused their opponents of being nativists and bigots. The opponents of prohibition also effectively argued that religion had no place in politics. "That Rayner letter and the presence of Bishop Turner, apparently carrying out in good faith its recommendations, needs, nay, demands explanation," wrote an antiprohibition editor. "Politics which mix up religions like that are dark and peculiar, and Dr. Carroll ought not to be in the business." Unlike Rayner, many African Americans could not see beyond the immediate issue of prohibition to the larger need to divide the Democratic Party. Black Republican leaders such as J. C. Akers of McKinney and Melvin Wade of Dallas stumped East Texas in the service of the antiprohibitionists, speaking at wet rallies and meeting Rayner in debate. Their arguments were simple but effective. Drawing upon the natural oratorical ability and keen sense of humor that would later make him an effective speaker for Populism, Wade told audiences that "he was a Republican because he was built that way, but if it was necessary in order to secure his personal right to take care of his own stomach to go with the Democrats he would go straight and as quick as a flash of lightning into the very middle of their camp." Wade and Akers portrayed prohibition as an attempt to curtail the personal liberties that African Americans had only enjoyed for the few brief years since emancipation.

Perhaps without realizing it, Wade and other wets occasionally touched upon the real reason for Rayner's ardent support of prohibition. When Wade made excuses for siding with the Democratic Party, he was tacitly admitting that prohibition struck a blow at the Democrats. Another antiprohibitionist was more explicit, openly charging Carroll with "doing his best to build up a third party, which, if established, will destroy the Democracy." The most telling accusation came from the antiprohibitionist editor of the *Wills Point Chronicle,* who described the typical prohibitionist as a "Prohib-Radical-Greenbacker-Disaffected-Political-Failure." Whether they knew it or not, the combatants in the 1887 prohibition campaign were fighting over something of far greater long-term importance than the right to take a drink. They were fighting over an issue which, if decided in favor of the prohibitionists, could deal a crippling blow to the Democratic Party and thus, presumably, to white supremacy. If no one else understood this fact in 1887, John B. Rayner did.

The voters of Texas went to the polls on August 4 and buried prohibition by a 90,000-vote majority. After the results were known, the jubilant wets made it clear that those prohibitionists who had thought they could disrupt the Democratic Party had been sorely mistaken; destroying the Democratic Party was no business for amateurs. As one antiprohibition editor pointedly expressed to B. H. Carroll, "You will greatly oblige us by taking as text for your Sunday sermon: 'Blessed is he that sitteth down on a hot gridiron, for he shall rise again.'" In a more serious vein, the editor of the *Examiner* asked rhetorically where certain prohibitionists would find their future political home. Answering his own question, the editor confessed to be unsure. But he predicted that any future movement seeking to divide the Democratic Party would "enjoy the embraces" of Rayner, Carroll, and other prohibitionists. In the case of Rayner, that prediction could not have been more correct.

The year 1887 would have been eventful for Rayner even without a heated political campaign. Sometime prior to the canvass, probably in 1886, his wife Susan had fallen seriously ill and died. A few days after the prohibition referendum, Rayner was arrested in Calvert on charges that he had raped Lizzie Anderson, a black schoolteacher. The assault was alleged to have taken place in mid-July. "The case evicted [*sic*] quite an interest," according to the *Galveston News,* because of the defendant's "notoriety during the late election campaign." Soon after the courts settled the matter in Rayner's favor, he was accosted in a Calvert store by Dennis Anderson, the woman's father. Anderson came at Rayner with a large knife, but as he lunged, the stoutly built politician picked up a chair and hurled it at his assailant. The chair struck Anderson in the arm that held the knife, causing a serious self-inflicted wound. Rayner "then ran for dear life, with Anderson a close second." The chase proceeded out of the store and down the busy street, until Rayner ducked into a livery stable. The stable's owner intervened and bravely brought the chase to an end.

The full story of this episode will never be known. The records of the Robertson County district court are complete for the period, but since they contain no mention of charges or a trial, the case almost certainly was dismissed. The "court room," which the press reported was "well filled with spectators," must have been either the preliminary hearing held by the justice of the peace or a grand jury hearing. One thing is beyond doubt: the outcome would have been drastically different had the alleged rape victim been a white woman. But in this case, the racial double-standard practiced by the South's legal system worked in Rayner's favor; black-on-black crime might elicit some curiosity from whites, but it did not invite the lynch mob.

Rayner, recently made a widower and sharing his father's passionate nature, may indeed have been involved with Lizzie Anderson; we will never know. What we do know is that less than three months after these events, Rayner married his late wife's younger sister, Clarissa, who had come down to Calvert from Tarboro to care for Susan during her illness. Until Rayner's death over thirty years later, the marriage between him and Clarissa would be strong and stable. Clarissa never complained, though she had to shoulder the heavy burdens of children, financial hardship, an often-exasperating husband, and a society that doubly oppressed those who were both black and female. She outlived her husband by forty-three years, dying in her Calvert home in 1961 at the age of 106.

Following the prohibition debacle, Rayner temporarily dropped from the political scene. He probably had to work harder than ever at teaching school in order to make ends meet, for Texas was experiencing some of the hardest economic times in the state's history. The years 1885–1887 had witnessed the most severe drought in anyone's memory. The price of cotton had sunk to 8.6 cents a pound, and with each passing year farmers found themselves more deeply ensnared in the crop lien system, whereby they were forced to mortgage their crops to "furnishing merchants" who provided supplies and provisions for the year. All too often crop prices fell, the merchant got the crop, and the farmer only fell further into debt. As bleak as the horizon looked for white farmers, African Americans' prospects seemed even dimmer. The great majority of adult black males in Texas were poor tenant farmers, and a gradual hardening of racial attitudes on the part of whites accompanied the deepening agricultural depression. In 1889 the state passed a law allowing separate railroad coaches for blacks, and the next legislature made segregated cars mandatory. Even more disturbing was the escalating rate at which Texas blacks who were accused of crimes met their fate at the hands of lynch mobs. One estimate placed the number of lynchings in the state at twenty-two for the year 1890 alone.

Rayner followed these disturbing developments from his home in Calvert, uncertain of the proper political course to pursue. African Americans in Texas had been more successful than their counterparts in many other southern states in retaining their right to vote, but by this time the traditional champion of black interests, the Republican Party, had become "a nonentity," as Rayner so aptly put it. Agrarian discontent lay smoldering just beneath the surface of Texas politics, but the abortive Greenback campaigns of the previous decade had provided little cause for encouragement. Rayner realized that political cooperation between downtrodden blacks and whites was not merely desirable; it was a practical necessity if the long reign of the Democrats was to broken. But how was such biracial cooperation to be achieved when racism was so ingrained in white culture? Most white Texans agreed with the influential East Texas Democratic congressman Roger Q. Mills when he stated, "the emancipation of the negro was a merciful, and, we believe, providential, affair; but clothing him with political privileges and power was a thing of satanic origin and consummation."

At the end of the 1880s Rayner could look back over the first forty years of his life and see—as clearly as anyone in America could—the ways in which white supremacy had disfigured the political life of the nation. The politics of race had destroyed the pre–Civil War party system, and in the 1860s it had nearly destroyed the nation itself. In the 1870s John B. Rayner had participated in the attempted restoration of the two-party system to the South via Radical Reconstruction. But the South's determination to preserve white supremacy doomed the chances of the Republicans to remain viable competitors in the system. As the Democratic Party consolidated its hold on the South in the 1870s and 1880s, Rayner was forced to make a choice. He could take a serious political gamble and affiliate with a new party, or he could acquiesce in the rule of a party that he knew would bring ruin to his people. There could be little doubt which choice he would make.

# CHAPTER THREE
## *The Promise of Populism*

BLACK POLITICAL AFFAIRS in Texas had reached a critical juncture by the early 1890s. Like other African Americans, John B. Rayner had shared in the lofty optimism of the Reconstruction years, only to see the Democrats systematically destroy African Americans' hopes for a just biracial society in the South. The Republican Party, once the champion of black rights, was impotent after the end of Reconstruction. Independent politics of the Greenbacker variety had invariably failed to produce lasting reform.

As Rayner sought some avenue that would lead to meaningful change, he could not help but notice the progress of the latest farmers' organization in the South, the Farmers' Alliance. Poor white farmers had increasingly found themselves cast into the same dire economic plight as most blacks, mired in tenancy and hopelessly indebted to the furnishing merchants. Led by a brilliant neighbor of Rayner's from nearby Milam County, Charles W. Macune, the Alliance numbered at least 100,000 members in Texas by 1887. A parallel organization for blacks, the Colored Farmers' Alliance, also enjoyed rapid growth. Originally a nonpartisan organization, the Alliance recognized the collective nature of the farmers' problems and thus sought to aid farmers by establishing cooperative purchasing and marketing ventures. When these private efforts ran headlong into the opposition of powerful business and financial interests, the Alliance began edging closer and closer toward insurgent politics. If such insurgency were to assume a biracial character, it would find an ally in John Rayner.

By 1890 the Alliance was a national organization, and in a series of state and national conventions it framed a list of political "demands" calling for government regulation or ownership of the railroads, abandonment of the gold standard in favor of both paper money and silver, equalization of the tax burden, prohibition of alien land ownership, and a graduated income tax. At the heart of the Alliance program was the Subtreasury Plan, a proposed federal network of warehouses that would store farmers' crops, extend guaranteed low-interest farm loans, and release the crops onto the world market in an orderly fashion, preventing the usual market glut—and depressed prices paid for farm commodities—come harvest time. The Subtreasury Plan would also go a long way toward solving the farmers' most pressing problem, the usurious short-term credit that had previously been available only through the furnishing merchants. At the same time it would increase the money supply, causing inflation and enabling debt-ridden farmers to meet their staggering financial obligations more easily. When the Alliance eventually formed its own independent political movement—the Populist, or People's, Party—these demands would form the heart of its platform.

The agrarian movement that produced the Alliance and People's Party was an attempt on the part of southern farmers to restore Jeffersonian principles to a rapidly industrializing and urbanizing nation. Populists tended to be small landowners fearful of losing their land and thus losing the personal independence that Jeffersonian ideology so highly valued. They rarely questioned the concept of private property, the need for commerce and manufacturing, or capitalism broadly defined, but they longed for a return to a simple market economy in which the "producers" of wealth—especially farmers—controlled the marketing of their goods and thus received full value for their labor. Although the solutions they proposed required an unprecedented rethinking of the role of government, Populists like Rayner did not see themselves as radicals; instead, they described their party as the home of true conservatism, for they saw themselves as the guardians of basic American values that monopolistic combinations (such as railroads, banks, and corporations) had endangered. They called for the workers of America to take control of their government away from the wealthy monopolists (and the politicians who served them) and begin using the power of the government to serve the interests of the laboring masses. Unlike modern conservatives, they saw no inherent conflict between an activist government and democracy, as long as that government's power rested in the hands of the people and was used to promote democratic values.

Rayner was not present in 1891 when a group of fifty Alliancemen met at a Dallas working-class hotel to organize the Texas People's Party, but he would soon realize the significance of what they had done. The delegates to that convention endorsed the demands that had been ironed out over the preceding several years by the Alliance. They also debated political strategy, confronting the issue that many must have dreaded but that had to be addressed: how was the party to handle the "Negro question"? The Populists could not afford simply to ignore African Americans, because in close races where the white vote was evenly divided, the black vote could mean the difference between victory and defeat. On the other hand, for Populists to appear too cozy with blacks would alienate thousands of potential white supporters and subject the new party to the same charges of racial infidelity that had always plagued the Republicans. The delegates in Dallas could not have avoided the issue if they had wanted to, because a handful of blacks there pressed the issue. Melvin Wade, a black labor leader and Republican activist from Dallas who had been one of Rayner's opponents in the prohibition campaign of 1887, demanded to know whether the new party intended "to work a black and a white horse in the same field." When the whites answered his questions with platitudes, Wade apparently left. But later in the day another African American, R. H. Hayes of Fort Worth, continued to press the Populists. Hayes, who had been active in independent politics in the 1880s, believed that rural blacks would eagerly "affiliate with any party against monopolies in the interest of the poor man." However, the new party would have to demonstrate good faith by placing blacks in positions of party leadership; "otherwise, as regards the colored vote," Hayes warned, "the streams would be poisoned."

In immediate terms, this meant black representation on the state executive committee was necessary. Committee chairman Harrison Sterling Price "Stump" Ashby made the most persuasive speech in favor of the proposal. "You are approaching a battlefield in which many errors have been made in the past," the eloquent Ashby told the delegates. "The Democrats have never given those [black] people representation; they have said they would buy enough of their votes with liquor and money. The Republicans have left the negro without a party. If he has a friend it is we, and he can be our friend. . . . We want to do good to every citizen of the country, and he is a citizen just as much as we are, and the party that acts on that fact will gain the colored vote of the south." Ashby's call for "full representation" brought forth applause from the assembled delegates. When one final attempt was made to dodge the issue by appointing blacks to cooperate with whites (rather than electing them outright to the executive committee), Hayes again took the floor. "You will lose in spite of the devil and high water if you do not treat the nigger squarely," he bluntly warned the Populists. Faced with this ultimatum, and having the support of leading whites such as Ashby, the new party took the bold step of electing two African Americans to the state executive committee.

The 1891 Dallas meeting was small and represented only a fraction of the state's Alliancemen. Whether or not it would produce a major third-party movement was still a question in many Texans' minds. Men of both races would have to be educated about the new party—such as who its leaders were, what its platform meant, and along what lines it was to be organized at the state and local levels. For those who had not closely followed the evolution of the Alliance, it could be confusing even to understand where it stood in relation to the People's Party. Did the Alliance support the third party or not? The confusion existing in the fall of 1891 is illustrated in John B. Rayner's initial approach to the new party. Populism apparently had not yet come to Robertson County. A few weeks after the Dallas convention, Rayner wrote Alliance leader Charles Macune a curious letter, explaining that since blacks "will not vote with the Demo-crats," perhaps "the best thing that we can do is to organize them into Knights of Labor" (the nation's leading labor union). While there is no evidence that the two men had previously met or corresponded, Rayner clearly recognized that Macune had achieved a preeminent position as the architect of the Alliance economic program—espe-cially with the innovative Subtreasury Plan. But Rayner apparently mistook Macune, who wished to wage the struggle from within the Democratic Party, as a proponent of third-party action. In his letter Rayner explained that African Americans were "anxious to identify themselves with the labor party." He claimed to have 150 men under his control who were "ready for organization," and he asked Macune to refer him to the proper authorities who could initiate them into a Knights of Labor chapter. The Knights of Labor had long sympa-thized with the Farmers' Alliance, but Rayner's purpose was not to begin unionizing black farmers *per se*. Instead, organizing his fol-lowers into a Knights chapter seemed to be the best way to "iden-tify" his people with the new third-party political movement. His mention of the "labor party" probably was a reference to the People's Party; Rayner simply did not know its proper name yet or how it was to be organized.

By the next year nobody in Texas had trouble knowing what to call the third party or identifying its leaders. Rayner began working for the Populist cause among the blacks of Robertson and the sur-rounding counties; and even Melvin Wade finally turned his back on twenty-five years of Republicanism and affiliated with the new move-ment. When the state convention of the People's Party met in 1892 to choose its first slate of state candidates, a few black Populists in South Texas brought encouraging stories of their success in recruiting Afri-can Americans to the party. "The colored people are coming into the new party in squads and companies," one black organizer reported. The Populists gave their gubernatorial nomination to Judge Thomas L. Nugent of Fort Worth, a quiet, scholarly man with an impeccable reputation as a champion of independent reform politics. The state Democratic Party split into two factions, with the conservative "Bour-bon" Democrats nominating railroad attorney George Clark and the "progressive," or reform, Democrats supporting the incumbent governor James S. Hogg, who had first won election on his promise to regulate the railroads. The fall elections would provide the new party with its first test of how successful it had been in spreading the agrarian gospel.

Rayner and the Populists faced huge obstacles in their first campaign. Not least among those obstacles was the resistance of the state's Republican Party. In a cynical attempt to defeat Hogg and gain a share of the spoils, the Republicans, led by the eminent black politician Norris Wright Cuney, endorsed the Democrat Clark. This marriage of convenience between the black Republicans and the Bourbon Democrats embittered Rayner and thousands of other blacks. "The Cuney Republicans," Rayner subsequently wrote, "are 95 per cent negroes and 5 per cent whites. The negroes in this party are hotel flunkies, barbers, dude school teachers, ignorant preachers, saloon waiters, etc." Though a teacher and preacher himself, he had clearly been influenced by the idea, common in Jeffersonian thought, that those lacking sufficient intelligence and virtue made poor voters and citizens. His unflattering description of black Republicans also suggests that Rayner had accepted the Populist notion that "producers" (farmers and workers) occupied a special place in American society—as opposed to those who earned their living in less socially beneficial ways.

White Populists wanted and needed to win black votes, but they appealed for those votes in a haphazard and halting fashion. Although the Populist program clearly addressed the economic needs of all poor farmers, the 1892 state platform made no specific mention of blacks. The document *did* address several issues of interest to the poor of both races: a plank demanding a six-month public school term with state-furnished textbooks was a significant improvement over Texas's grossly inadequate public school system. Farmers and laborers would benefit from the party's proposal of a more equitable lien law that would prevent tools and other productive assets from seizure by creditors. The party called for reforms in the notorious convict lease system, which turned convicts (a disproportionate number of whom were black) into virtual slaves for the duration of their sentences.

And the Populists' demand for fair elections, if carried out, would strike a blow at the Democrats' time-honored practice of stealing elections that they could not win fairly.

But as meaningful as these proposed reforms were, the People's Party kept silent on many of the most pressing of African Americans' concerns. It failed to condemn lynching, which had claimed as many as forty victims in Texas during some recent years. No mention was made of the 1889 state law that segregated railroad cars, the blatant discrimination in state expenditures for black schools, or the right of blacks to sit on juries. With one Democratic candidate (the incumbent Hogg) on record against lynching, and with the other candidate (Clark) enjoying the endorsement of Cuney's Republicans, the Populists stood little chance of success among the masses of Texas blacks. The naming of blacks to the Populist state executive committee and a general appeal to economic self-interest were all that most blacks could see as a benefit of Populism. These Populist gestures, along with the prospect of defeating the Democrats, were sufficient to attract Rayner in 1892, but they were not enough to convert the black masses to Populism.

The 1892 election returns revealed the failure of Rayner and the Populists to attract black voters as well as the Populists' inability to woo sufficient numbers of whites away from the Democratic Party. The state ticket headed by Nugent finished a distant third behind Democrats Hogg and Clark. Populists received very little black support. Black voters fell into three roughly equal groups, with one-third supporting Hogg, another third voting for Clark, and the remainder staying at home. Clearly, large numbers of blacks were disgusted with the choice of either Hogg or Clark, but they could see no good reason to vote for the Populist Nugent.

In the wake of the 1892 defeat, the People's Party had to reexamine its strategy. Populist voting was centered in the predominantly white frontier farming counties of north-central Texas, with a few pockets of strength in some of the poorer piney-woods regions of the east. The party carried very few of the plantation regions in which large numbers of African American sharecroppers lived. In many of these areas the black-dominated Republican Party continued to pose a threat to white control, and thus whites were very reluctant to split their vote between the Populist and Democratic parties and risk getting blacks in office. African Americans were just as hesitant to desert the Republican Party—the party of Lincoln and emancipation— and entrust their fate to a group of white southerners. The Populists had to find a way to make both blacks and whites in the Black Belt place reform ahead of racial anxieties. The third party needed to show white Democrats that the desperate financial plight of farmers would never improve under Democratic rule and that whites and blacks could honorably cooperate for the common good without engendering "social equality" for African Americans. Populists also had to convince blacks that they were sincere in offering them meaningful political participation. There were good reasons to be optimistic about the chances of recruiting more white Populists as the agricultural depression deepened. Cotton prices over the next two years would plummet to less than a nickel a pound, below the break-even point for even the most efficient farmer. Many whites were already familiar with Populist demands via the Farmers' Alliance and the rapidly growing reform press. But black "Pop clubs" could not organize themselves, and few blacks could read (or afford) newspapers that would instill in them the vital education of Populism. The party needed to address black issues more directly and find more blacks with leadership ability, courage, and dedication to travel and work tirelessly as organizers and educators.

Rayner had maintained a low profile during the 1892 election, restricting his activities to some local speechmaking in the vicinity of Robertson County. But events in his home county provided a political education that shaped his actions for the remainder of the Populist revolt. Robertson County in 1892 manifested many of the factors required to bring success to a local Populist organization. First, the local black political hierarchy was already in tune with the rising agrarian sentiment of the early 1890s. Not only had blacks and whites achieved an unusually high degree of solidarity in the Greenback campaigns of the prior decade, but the county appears to have been a stronghold of the Colored Farmers' Alliance. Black Alliancemen in

Calvert inaugurated a newspaper called the *Alliance Vindicator* in February 1892. Alex Asberry, the leading black Republican politician of the county, apparently edited the paper and served as state president of the Colored Farmers' Alliance. Second, a relatively small but influential group of white Democrats abandoned their party and proved eager to form a working partnership with the blacks. This movement apparently began with the June 1892 resignation from the Democratic Party of Calvert's E. S. Peters.

Peters, who became one of Rayner's most important white allies in the People's Party, was one of the more enterprising men of turn-of-the-century Texas. A native of Michigan, he had come to Texas at the age of twenty and married the daughter of James K. Polk Hanna, a wealthy planter from Calvert. Peters eventually acquired thousands of acres of land and served many years as president of the Texas chapter of the American Cotton Growers' Association. In June 1892 Peters tendered his resignation as chairman of the Fourteenth Senatorial District's Democratic committee. In a public resignation statement he harshly indicted the Democratic Party, which he claimed had been led "away from the fundamental principles of the democracy upon which our free institutions were founded and [had been] delivered to the oppressive money and corporate powers which have corrupted its leaders and now control the party." Peters and his father-in-law Hanna, along with Rayner, became the leaders of Populism in Robertson County, and in 1892 the district's Populists nominated Peters for state senator and Hanna for presidential elector.

As the fall elections approached, Peters, Hanna, Rayner, and other local Populists began collaborating with black Republicans such as Alex Asberry. In the first week of September the Populists held a two-day rally at the county fairgrounds in Calvert, featuring speeches by Nugent and lesser Populist personalities. Local black leaders soon were warning blacks about "being made a tool of by designing office seekers" and urging them "to vote for intelligent and respectable men of their own party or else join with the leading white citizens in their efforts in behalf of good government." The Republicans subsequently endorsed Peters and several other local Populist nominees but refused to support Populist gubernatorial nominee Thomas Nugent.

When election returns were counted, it was quite apparent what had transpired in Rayner's home county. The inability of the Republicans and Populists to agree on a joint gubernatorial ticket had resulted in a victory for the conservative Democrat George Clark, but in contests such as the congressional race, where the Republicans endorsed the Populist candidate, the third party won with 54 percent of the county's vote. Returns from the entire county are incomplete, but at the Calvert box—the center of fusionist strength with a large black vote—the white Populist candidates for district attorney and district judge swamped their Democratic opponents by a three-to-one margin.

From the vantage point of Robertson County, Rayner could easily read the lesson of 1892; something very new was afoot in southern politics. A party of white native southerners who opposed Democrats of all stripes appeared anxious to allow blacks to participate in shaping party policy. Rayner could look at his home county and see the formula for success: find brave whites like Peters and Hanna who were not afraid to desert the hallowed Democratic Party, convert every possible poor white and black farmer to the new cause, and convince the Republicans as a party to enter into an alliance with Populists to defeat the entrenched Democrats. He believed that success at the polls and the realization of justice in government, combined with continuing education and agitation, would soon render Populist-Republican fusion unnecessary. As blacks began to receive a fair break from the Populist state government, they would leave the Party of Lincoln as Rayner himself had done. Blacks could be persuaded to vote a straight People's Party ticket, Rayner at one point stated, if only the Populists would "put men on the precinct and county tickets whom he (the negro) likes." The local level was the key. "Kind words and just treatment" from Populists in the precinct and county would eventually translate into statewide victories.

Rayner and the Populists found ample reason for encouragement in the wake of their defeat, despite the fact that they had finished third in the statewide races. The party sent eight of its men to the state legislature in 1892 and, as in Robertson County, scored numerous victories at the local level. In Calvert, Peters began publishing a Populist newspaper, the *Citizen-Democrat*, and he accurately reported in 1893 that "Populist papers are springing up like mushrooms." Populism was spreading with astonishing rapidity. By the following year the third party was prepared to mount a serious challenge to the now nervous Democrats, and Rayner was poised on the brink of a remarkable career.

As the 1894 campaign heated up, the state Populist press, the metropolitan dailies, and numerous small Democratic weeklies began to note the political activities of a "traveling negro named Rayner." In March of that year the *Texas Advance,* the state paper of the People's Party, started publishing speaking schedules of "Rev. J. B. Rayner, colored, our Populist orator." Typically Rayner would visit a county and speak at black barbecues, picnics, and political meetings or conventions. Sometimes he made his speeches at the county courthouse or a local opera house, sometimes in tiny, off-the-beaten-path black settlements. He publicly offered his services to any county Populist organization that needed them. "I will now gladly visit any part of the state," he proclaimed in the *Advance,* "and organize my people into Populist clubs. Address me at Calvert, Texas." Announcements for his speaking engagements invited "all who favor justice, liberty, a higher price for labor, and a better price for products."

The responses were overwhelming. In April, May, and June 1894 Rayner crisscrossed the eastern half of the state, speaking to crowds of all sizes and descriptions, leaving behind a trail of black Populist clubs and consummating local fusion agreements between Populists and Republicans. Driven by the vital issues at stake—or simply curious—rural Texans of both races gathered to see and hear the man who was billed as the "Silver-Tongued Orator of the Colored Race." The following report, coming from a Populist partisan in a small town near Austin, is typical: "The colored people of Elgin turned out in masse [sic] on last Saturday to hear J. B. Rayner of Calvert, our Populist orator. The opera house was filled with white and black, and Rayner made many colored Populists by his address. We are growing in numbers and influence."

Rayner himself frequently took time to report his successes to the Populist faithful. One such letter provides a glimpse into Rayner's power as a speaker and the idealism that suffused the efforts of Texas's black Populists:

"I have fought a good fight and have kept the faith," and by telling the truth converted to our political ideas every colored man and woman in Jasper and Newton counties. I have converted at least fifty percent of my white auditors. The people in this part of the state are anxious for the truth, and I have told it to them and am proud of my work.

When I first came to these two counties the Democrats tried to hire a little pride-intoxicated colored school teacher to follow and reply to me, and so when I spoke at Jasper he came to reply and commenced to take notes of my argument, and when I had finished my talk, I found that he was nailed to his seat, and from now on he is out of politics.

The people in Jasper and Newton counties are virtuous and brave, and all they need is the light and truth.

Of course, thunderous oratory and "light and truth" alone would not win statewide campaigns. Rayner knew that the poverty of most Populists and the pitfalls inherent in interracial cooperation called for a well-thought-out strategy. Education was a vital part of that strategy. Rayner worked closely with white orators and with the reform press, making recommendations to his white comrades about where their services were needed and helping poor blacks and whites obtain copies of Populist newspapers. He rarely hesitated to instruct his white colleagues on how to run a campaign, giving detailed directions in the state Farmer's Alliance paper, the *Southern Mercury,* for the benefit of county and precinct Populist leaders. Above all, he stressed to white Populists the need to utilize his own services and to enlist local black leaders in the Populist cause. "Our county chairmen in counties where the negro vote is important, should have colored speakers to visit the county, and address and instruct the colored voters," Rayner wrote. "You must reach the negro through a negro. This is possible with the People's party, but impossible with the Democracy . . . . The negro is a silent spectator. He never had any confidence in the Democratic Party, and he has lost confidence in the Republican Party, and this is written, because I know what must be done to get the negro's vote."

Rayner's activities almost always invited controversy. In Freestone County he was "circulating among the colored people" two weeks before the local Populist nominating convention. The Democratic *Fairfield Recorder* reported that Rayner led the county's black Republicans to believe "that if they would unite with the Populists they should have two commissioners and a county office." When the convention met and a black delegate allegedly pressed Rayner to make good on the promise, Rayner reportedly denied the existence of any such deal. A local Populist paper gave a very different account of the events. The *Wortham Vindicator* said that the report of Rayner having promised blacks offices "was emphatically false. . . . But we did offer to seat them in convention and did seat colored delegates from five precincts and allowed them to help us name our ticket."

The Democratic editor grudgingly admitted the truth of the *Vindicator*'s statement. Then, in a revealing flourish of hypocrisy, he scornfully editorialized, "'Helped us name our ticket.' How munificent, how noble in the Pops! The colored delegates were not permitted to mention their ticket, but 'they helped us nominate our ticket.' Then, to smooth things over, they gave the colored brother a 'resolution,' allowing them equal right to sit on juries." Rayner obviously had been walking a political tightrope in Freestone, trying to do justice to his fellow blacks without jeopardizing the party's chances among whites. But whether or not he actually promised African Americans specific offices—which is doubtful—the Democratic editor unfairly charged the Populists with exploiting blacks. Not only did the third party grant them a voice in the nominations, but the resolution favoring blacks on juries captured the heart of the Populist racial appeal. As long as whites controlled the apparatus of southern courts, they could hold the terrible prospect of the convict lease system over the heads of black sharecroppers, thus maintaining an oppressive labor system that bore an uncomfortable resemblance to slavery. To the white Democratic editor entrenched in a political culture where spoils were the principal object of politics, allowing blacks "equal right to sit on juries" was simply a way "to smooth things over." To African Americans, ending Democratic hegemony over the court system was an issue of paramount importance.

In the months following Rayner's initial organization of Freestone County blacks, Populist candidates in the county repeatedly emphasized what Populism could mean to African Americans. Speaking two months later at a black barbecue, L. N. Barbee, the district's Populist state representative, told a black audience, "You all know the Democrats never have allowed you a voice in their conventions and they never will. Because we seated you in our county convention and allowed you a voice in naming our candidates, every Democrat in Freestone county just harped on it." The white Populist then asked the blacks a pointed question: "How many of you have ever sat on a jury? Do you suppose that if I were jerked up down here at Fairfield to be tried before a jury that I would want a jury of lawyers, doctors and highly educated men? No, sir, I would demand a jury of farmers who till the soil as I do, men of my equal. You have the same privilege and ought to be allowed a voice in selecting a jury of your equals." Rayner had brought the word of Populism to Freestone County's black Republicans; it was then up to the local white Populist leaders like Barbee to establish a working coalition with them.

Due in large measure to Rayner's work, the profile of black Populism was changing. Since the disastrous 1892 showing among blacks, Populism steadily had been winning converts. By the time the 1894 state convention met at Waco, both blacks and whites felt that real progress was being made in attracting blacks to the People's Party. At previous conventions African Americans had been conspicuous mainly because of their scarcity, but the 1894 meeting saw them participating in Populism in much greater numbers. None played a more prominent role in the convention's proceedings than the former North Carolinian.

Rayner and some twelve hundred delegates converged on Waco on the evening of June 19 for the 1894 state convention. The next morning the delegates made their way to a city park, where the Waco Commercial Club had provided a huge tent for the convention. The charismatic Stump Ashby, whose former occupations included that of actor, opened the meeting with a hymn, followed by a prayer. There can be no doubt that many of the delegates viewed the coming campaign more in terms of a holy war than a political contest. The first hours of the convention were spent in speechmaking by the party's heavyweights, including Ashby and James H. "Cyclone" Davis, a spellbinding orator. But before long, several African Americans also addressed the gathering. The total number of black delegates is not known, but on the convention's first day the *Waco Evening News* reported that "the colored brother was a conspicuous figure and seemed to know what he was there for . . . a hearty welcome was accorded him."

Rayner was among the more conspicuous African Americans at the Waco convention. On the first day Ashby introduced him to the delegates. A correspondent for the *San Antonio Express* reported that few in the audience knew he was black when he approached the speakers' stand. Rayner commenced his brief address with a joke that he never failed to use with great effect in his stump speeches. Making fun of white southerners' professed abhorrence of miscegenation, he facetiously explained that the Democratic Party (which had dominated southern politics in the era when his slaveholder father had sired him) "was responsible for his complexion." Rayner then echoed what had become a familiar theme with him; he told the Populists that if they meant to help black people, they should "let the dude school teachers and long-tailed preachers alone." Rayner recognized that the black political power in the South traditionally had rested in the hands of teachers and ministers. He believed that in their blind allegiance to the Republican Party or in kowtowing to Democrats, black teachers and ministers had too often abused the trust that many black people placed in them. But this would be no more. From now on, Rayner assured his audience, black Texans would "look . . . to the third party for their salvation."

Throughout the convention African Americans mounted the podium to proclaim the new gospel of Populism. Their message always revolved around a common theme: the dire economic hardships being endured by both poor blacks and poor whites and the mistreatment of both races at the hands of the old parties. African American politician Melvin Wade, now firmly in the Populist camp, echoed this theme when he, too, addressed the convention on the first day. In the 1891 convention Wade had asked whether the People's Party intended "to work a black and a white horse in the same field." With characteristic humor, he now told the 1,200 Populists that the "Democratic and Republican parties are just alike. They hitch up the white man and the nigger together and drive 'em together just like the man here in this town I see drivin' a white and a black horse. If one of them stops and don't want to pull—don't make no difference which one it is, white or black—he lays on the whip." The Republican Party, Wade argued, had "been treating the nigger just like the hunter treats his dogs. Snaps its finger and they jump and bark, then does this way (motioning down with his hand) and they lay down for four years. . . ." With the delegates in stitches, Rayner's black comrade ridiculed the "Young feller [who] says he's a Democrat because his father was one. According to him I ought to want to be a slave because my father was one."

The high point of the meeting came on the second day, when the Populists nominated their candidates for state offices. In a dramatic moment, they placed the name of Judge Thomas L. Nugent in nomination for governor. Then, at the peak of the convention's euphoria, Rayner took the floor to second the nomination. The "colored delegate from Robertson" made an eloquent plea for interracial cooperation, diplomatically proclaiming that African Americans "had endured 4000 years of savagery and 245 years of slavery, only to find that the white man of the south is the negro's first, best and firmest friend." His voice ringing, Rayner urged the Populists to "Nominate Nugent and the negro will be as faithful to your flag as he was to your wives and children when you were fighting the battles of your country." Masterfully appealing to the Confederate tradition without downplaying the fact that slavery was an evil blacks had endured, Rayner's speech was met with loud applause by the enthusiastic delegates, who proceeded to nominate Nugent by acclamation.

On the third morning of the convention the delegates faced two remaining tasks: selecting a new executive committee to serve for the next two years and adopting an official platform. Rayner, now clearly the chief spokesman for the black Populists, was elected committeeman from the state at-large and took his place on the fifteen-man board. Perhaps equally important, Rayner was named to the platform committee. That afternoon the platform committee met from noon until almost 6 o'clock in the evening. Although reportedly "a long war was waged in the committee over the platform," the committee "presented an unbroken front when they entered the big tent." The platform was adopted with near unanimity by the delegates. No Populist platform ever contained the sweeping civil rights declarations that would come along seventy years later. Yet the platforms of the Texas People's Party in the 1890s contained a number of planks that clearly addressed the interests of black Americans. Like its predecessor two years earlier, the 1894 platform included planks demanding major reforms in the brutal convict lease system. The Populists proposed first that "convict labor be taken out of competition with citizens['] labor," a practice which everyone knew held down the wages of the common laborer in Texas. If stringently enforced, such a law would also reduce the harshness of the system by reducing the immense profitability of exploiting convict labor. Second, the plank specified "that convicts be given intellectual and moral instructions, and that the earnings of the convict above the expenses of keeping him, should go to his family." Again the plank would go far in humanizing an exploitative institution that all too often victimized African Americans and their families.

Both the 1892 and 1894 state platforms included demands for "fair elections and an honest count," measures that would help guard against the fraud that had helped to keep the Democrats in power for twenty years. The 1894 platform also retained earlier planks calling for "an efficient lien law" to protect laboring men, an eight-hour work day for industrial workers, and the creation of a state board of arbitration to hear all disputes between corporations and employees. The 1894 platform, however, went beyond the provisions of the party's 1892 document in addressing blacks' interests. Attesting to the increasing influence of blacks in the party and the presence of Rayner on the platform committee, the new platform included two planks that specifically addressed racial issues. One of these was a demand that the state provide "sufficient accommodation for all its insane, without discrimination in color." The other involved public education, an issue that many blacks viewed as tremendously important.

The 1892 platform had favored a system of public schools with a six-month academic year, available to all children between the ages of six and twenty, and the adoption of standardized textbooks provided at no cost by the state. These demands, modest by modern standards, constituted a major improvement over the existing system of four-month school years and overpriced, inadequate texts. In 1894, however, the Populists went beyond these already substantial proposals by providing that "each race shall have its own trustees and control its own schools." More than any other feature of the platform, this provision bore Rayner's imprimatur; changing the governance of black public schools was an idea he championed for the rest of his life. Since much of the power of white supremacy rested upon the continued ignorance and illiteracy of blacks, taking control of black education away from the Democrats was of the utmost importance. The *Galveston Daily News* evaluated the effect of this new plank quite accurately: "This declaration appeals irresistibly to the colored brother. He fairly dotes on schools and the colored delegates enthusiastically declared that 50,000 Republican votes would land in the populist camp next November. They meant it, too. It remains to be seen whether or not they can deliver the goods, but there is no doubt about their sincerity. They will do their best."

Rayner certainly intended to do his best. The black Populists of Texas left the 1894 convention with higher spirits than ever before. A Democratic defeat at the hands of the Populists would not mean sudden equality for blacks; no one, black or white, pretended that it would. But it would mean the defeat of the South's most unequivocal champions of white supremacy and the accession to power of men who seemed honestly committed to republican principles. For Populist leaders like Rayner and Wade, that promise—huge in its significance for blacks in the year 1894—was enough.

Rayner left Waco and almost immediately commenced a wide-ranging speaking and organizing tour that threatened both his health and personal safety. A week after the convention he made five speeches in Polk County, followed by a thorough canvass of San Augustine, Nacogdoches, and Waller counties. He then ventured 200 miles to the north—unfamiliar territory for him—and spoke in Lamar, Red River, Bowie, and Morris counties. By early September he was back in the deep East Texas counties of San Augustine and Nacogdoches.

Late September found Rayner 200 miles to the southwest in Bastrop, Hays, and Comal counties, and by the first week in October he had spoken as far south as Jackson County on the Gulf Coast. "I am hard at work day and night for our party," he explained without exaggeration. The tireless orator was due back in Henderson County near Dallas the following week when the strain of his schedule landed him in the sickbed.

Rayner's experiences on the campaign trail in 1894 dramatically underscore the power of white supremacy and the lengths to which Democrats would go when they believed it to be endangered. The black orator displayed exceptional physical courage when venturing into certain parts of East Texas, literally joking about the threats he encountered. In Morris County, Rayner spoke to a crowd of 450 white and black Populists and reported that later that "night some of the Democrats that worship at the shrine of Bacchus [drunks] tried to frighten me and make me leave town. One poor little fellow wanted to know who would pay him to run 'that nigger' out of town." Rayner continued undeterred. While he did not elaborate further on the threat, he did add that "the colored people of Morris county are doing their own thinking and will vote with the Populists. . . . Our party is growing daily and I am cheerful, hopeful and feel that victory is waiting to crown our efforts. My people are . . . developing an individuality that will command the respect of all men. I am working night and day for Judge Nugent and our party."

The emerging alliance between black and white Populists tested the resolve of the white members as frequently as it did that of black members. In Polk County, for example, Populists were severely criticized by the local Democratic newspaper for inviting Rayner to lecture there. The Democrats accused the Populists of "promising the negroes to elect them to office, and advocating social equality . . . in order to get their votes." The local Populist convention simply responded by reminding the public that Democrats had always tried to deceive the people, and then they let the matter drop. In doing so, the Populists were in effect refusing to engage in racial demagoguery or to respond seriously to charges of treason to the white race. Such refusals took considerable courage in the racially heated atmosphere of the 1890s.

As Rayner's fame as an orator and his ability as a Populist organizer spread, the chances of racial conflict in the course of his speaking tours increased. In many Black Belt (plantation) areas, maintaining absolute white solidarity spelled the only hope of preventing the election of black Republicans. Populism threatened that solidarity by splitting the white vote. Racial tensions in such areas could boil over during election season. In July 1894, as Rayner was about to visit Waller County in the heart of the southeast Texas Black Belt, a racially charged incident took place. A healthy Populist organization in the county was making a strong bid for the black vote and had even placed an African American on the county ticket. Democrats feared a Republican or fusion victory. On July 10 rumors surfaced concerning a "race war" or "negro rising" in the Brazos river bottom. Soon sixty or seventy armed men formed a vigilante force and rode into the bottom, sending a large number of black families fleeing to the backwoods in terror. For several days all work in the fields came to a halt. In light of this activity, Rayner prudently postponed his speaking engagements, and the chairman of the county Populist organization directly charged the Democrats with starting the mischief in order to frighten blacks and lay the blame at the doorstep of the People's Party.

Ten days later, reports began to circulate on the streets of Hempstead that local Democrats had sent the black orator a telegram threatening his life if he came to the town to make a speech. The threat may have been nothing more than a rumor, because Rayner and the editors of the *Hempstead News* quickly took steps to dispel it. Whatever the case, Rayner took his chances with this volatile situation and made several speeches in Waller County. He spoke at the county courthouse to a large racially mixed audience, amid buoyant talk that a fusion deal would be consummated between the Populists and Republicans. Every one of the candidates from all parties attended the speech, but Rayner pulled no punches "in abusing the Democratic party." The local Democratic editor admitted the speaker's knowledge of Populist doctrine and his eloquence, comparing him favorably with star orators Stump Ashby and Cyclone Davis. As a prominent local Populist put it, "He is one of the hardest hitters I ever heard."

Except for his appearances at the party's state conventions and at the big summer Populist camp meetings, Rayner spent most of his time working at the grassroots level. He placed tremendous emphasis on mobilizing a county's black voters on behalf of Populist aspirants for county offices such as sheriff or county judge. He understood—perhaps better than many of the party's white leaders—the vital importance of this sort of local organization. Naturally he found ample opportunities to promote the candidacy of the party's state and national figures, but in Rayner's efforts these races usually took a second seat. As the 1894 elections drew nearer, however, managers of one congressional campaign recruited Rayner to work specifically in their candidate's behalf. Although historians have despaired over the fact that virtually no major Texas Populist candidate's or organizer's private papers have been preserved, one manuscript collection that provides a rare glimpse into Populist-era Texas politics in the state does survive. The papers of Vachel Weldon uniquely illuminate Rayner's career as well as the inner workings of Populist revolt in the Lone Star State.

Vachel Weldon ran for the U.S. House of Representatives in 1894 as an Independent, supported by a Republican-Populist "fusion" deal. His twenty-four county district, the Eleventh, encompassed all of South Texas but extended up the Gulf Coast in a northeasterly direction as far as Wharton County, one of the most heavily black regions of the state. The five counties bordering the Rio Grande contained large numbers of Mexican Americans and the middle counties varying mixes of whites, blacks, and Hispanics. Five of the upper counties were at least 20 percent black. The only counties with black majorities were Wharton (81 percent) and Jackson (56 percent). The district, like the state as a whole, contained pockets of Populist strength, but remained essentially Democratic and was easily expected to reelect the incumbent, William H. Crain. Corrupt Democratic bosses in the counties along the Rio Grande always made sure the Democrats won. The Republican Party historically garnered support from blacks in the northeastern counties and from German and Anglo-American sheep ranchers in the north-central counties. The best the Independent ticket could hope for in those areas was to keep what few honest Populist or Republican votes there were from being stolen. In the northern counties, however, the prospect appeared bright for Independent support sufficient to counteract the Democratic advantage in the south.

On October 1 a Populist leader from black-majority Jackson County wrote to Weldon explaining the situation in that locale. "You can carry this county by three fourths, the Republicans and Populists voting for you, but a great effort is being made to induce the negroes to vote the Democratic ticket," he warned. "And of course success in this regard will imperil your success." Here, in its barest form, was the equation that almost always determined Populist success in areas with a significant black population: neither Populists nor Republicans could expect to win on their own, but if they could combine their votes on one ticket and keep the black vote from landing in the Democratic column, the fusion ticket could carry the day. In the case of the Eleventh District, the first condition—fusion—was accomplished. Populists and Republicans were supporting Weldon. A white Populist leader of Jackson County thought he knew how to fulfill the second condition:

To counteract this [Democratic] influence we have a negro speaker who will hold the colored vote to the Republican [ticket], that he can not turn to the Populist side. I have heard him speak twice in this county, and he is the ablest speaker for the service I have ever heard. He carries such conviction by his appeals and arguments, that few colored men can resist. I am willing to pledge my reputation for a man of judgement upon what I say with regard to him. I am too old a man to allow any temporary enthusiasm to overcome my cooler judgement, and I tell you I have seen and heard him destroy all the effect of a strong Republican [or] Democratic speech in a single sentence, and turn over not only colored Republicans but white Democrats, nor were they slow to acknowledge it. You hear him first, and judge for yourself.

The writer was referring to Rayner. This letter, written in strict privacy and with great earnestness, indicates not only how devastatingly effective Rayner was as a speaker but how critically the

Populists needed his brand of articulate and skilled black leadership at the grassroots level. A related problem for the Populists was that of campaign finance; black leaders could not rely on their own personal wealth as could white elites. From 1894 to 1898 Rayner labored virtually full-time for the party but received no salary. Apart from the money his wife earned by taking in white people's laundry, he relied entirely on voluntary contributions from audiences, candidates, and white Populist leaders. The Weldon campaign had to address this problem if Rayner was to continue to do his work. This, according to a Weldon worker, was "the milk in the cocoanut: We want him [Rayner] in Calhoun, Victoria, DeWitt, Karnes, and Goliad counties, and we are as you know not very well equipped financially to employ speakers." This Populist offered to donate his salary as a gin superintendent to pay Rayner during the campaign, and he called on a neighboring county Populist chairman for added support. These donations, "with voluntary contributions from others," would enable the campaign to keep Rayner "at work until the campaign . . . ended." Then there would be "no doubt" that Weldon would "carry the counties of this senatorial dis[ric]t by so large a majority that the Democratic majorities of the Rio Grande counties will be annihilated."

Weldon did obtain Rayner's services, and by October 8 the black orator had delivered eight speeches, with at least seven more already scheduled. The Populists needed Rayner to stay longer, and he was willing to stay in the district until election day, but money was short. Weldon had sent him $25, but as Rayner argued, "what is this for a traveling speaker[?]" There were times during Populist campaigns when postage stamps with which to answer political correspondence imposed such a financial burden on Rayner that he had to request his correspondents to enclose stamps in their letters. And when Rayner had fallen ill earlier in the campaign, he publicly thanked his white hometown Populist ally, E. S. Peters, for a $10 donation. "It came at the right time," wrote Rayner.

The Populist-Republican alliance in the Eleventh District stretched its resources to the breaking point to finance Weldon's campaign. But in the dozens of surviving letters that tell of the campaign's financing, the picture emerges quite clearly: money was a necessity, and the Democrats had most of it. Certainly the Independents knew the game. One Weldon lieutenant in DeWitt County described how "two hundred dollars could be used here to a splendid advantage" in interesting the county's African American preachers and a German newspaper editor in Weldon's candidacy. However, such funds were small change compared to what was being spent by the Democrats in the Rio Grande Valley.

In the upper counties success continued to hinge upon Rayner's efforts to swing the black vote Weldon's way. A Weldon supporter in Goliad County reported that blacks there were solidly in favor of the Independent candidate, adding that "Rayner did more good for Weldon than all speakers combined who went to Goliad." But even with African Americans firmly lined up behind the Independent ticket, Weldon's forces in such counties had not definitely won the battle. Those black voters who refused to be bought were still subject to deception at the polls. Illiteracy ran high among black farmers, and the intricate election laws of the period could confuse all but the most educated and alert voters. Regulations required that ballots be printed on a certain type of paper, with a specific kind of ink, and folded in a particular way. Otherwise, Democratic election officials could throw them out on a technicality. Democrats practiced an even more common, and probably more successful, tactic of simply passing out Democratic ballots to the blacks and telling them they were Populist or Republican ballots. Therefore, while Rayner had performed his job admirably, the Independents still had to supervise black voting on election day. As a Weldon supporter explained, "All the Negroes are unconditional Weldon people but don't know who is to lead them & what I propose to do is to get men I can rely upon to give them the Weldon tickets on the day of election." With the election machinery in the hands of the Democrats, it was crucial that the opposition have trustworthy men at every polling place where blacks would be voting.

On the eve of the election, Weldon's backers were frantically trying to find ways to counteract the manipulation of black voters in the upper counties and the massive fraud expected in the Rio Grande counties. "Money is flying," an Hispanic Populist reported from South Texas, and the Populists had a mere $33 dollars left in the campaign chest. Despite the efforts of Rayner and his white allies, Weldon faced almost certain defeat.

When the votes were tallied, the fusion ticket had carried sixteen of the twenty-eight counties, nine of them by very large margins. In the five counties with greater than 20 percent black population, all of which Rayner had campaigned in, Weldon won 57 percent of the votes cast. In one of the black-majority counties (Jackson) where Rayner had been especially active, the fusion ticket polled 60 percent. But in the five Valley counties—Cameron, Hidalgo, Starr, Zapata, and Webb—Crain defeated Weldon by a margin of nearly three to one. Excluding the five counties along the Rio Grande from the twenty-eight-county totals, Weldon won easily with 55 percent of the vote. In one Valley county, Cameron, the lopsided Democratic majority was enough to prevent what would have been a Weldon victory district-wide.

Even seasoned veterans of the region's politics were shocked at the extent of the voting fraud. Democratic bosses naturalized large numbers of new citizens the day before the election to secure their votes. Multiple witnesses reported seeing officials at the polls opening ballot boxes and inspecting the ballots after they had been cast. Election judges allowed illegally marked ballots to stand. The Democrats brought hundreds of aliens in from Mexico for the day just to vote. Certain precincts voted more than their entire population. At one polling place, a man with a gun threatened voters. An outraged friend of Weldon's explained that there had been 2,000 fraudulent votes cast in three counties, "and the fact can be easily demonstrated." "All concealment was thrown aside," he explained, and Democratic politicians simply responded by saying, "What in hell are you going to do about it." Weldon's supporters urged him to "contest and contest vigorously," but despite overwhelming evidence of fraud his lawyer advised against it. Democrat William H. Crain was the next U.S. congressman from the Eleventh District.

Although the Mexican population and international border in many ways make the Eleventh District unique, the Weldon and Crain campaigns reveal much about Populism in general. First, Populist ideological principles under some circumstances could be sacrificed—at least in the short run—in order to achieve the greater goal of defeating the Democrats. (Weldon, it will be recalled, was an Independent running with Populist and Republican support.) Any Democratic defeat, even at the hands of a Republican or Independent, loosened the Democrats' grip in the election machinery, the justice system, and patronage, opening the door for future Populist achievements. Second, the black vote *could* be won without resorting to wholesale fraud, but this required black Populist leadership such as Rayner provided and reliable men at the precincts to make sure that blacks were not deceived. Finally, the election demonstrates the lengths to which Democrats would go to ensure victory. And while fraud was easier to perpetrate on the border, it was widespread across the state.

The 1894 state elections did not bring victory to the Populist state ticket, but in many respects Rayner and his comrades had cause to feel encouraged. With the Democrats reunited behind a single gubernatorial candidate and a Republican ticket again in the field, the election provided the best opportunity yet to gauge Populist strength. Nugent, once more the Populist gubernatorial candidate, finished second to the colorless Democrat Charles Culberson by a vote of 216,373 to 159,676. The Republicans and Prohibitionists polled a combined vote of 83,746. Nugent's vote had increased by over 50,000 since 1892. With the help of men like Rayner, Populism was growing in Texas.

By the end of 1894 John B. Rayner had built a remarkable political career. Not only was he the undisputed leader of Texas's black Populists, but he had earned the respect of many white leaders of the party. From his position on the Populist state executive committee he exercised genuine influence over party policy. The People's Party was still a long way from embracing true racial equality, but the progress was encouraging. Rayner could look to the not-too-distant future and see a time when Populism would triumph at the polls, and the nation would move closer to fulfilling its long-deferred promise of liberty and justice for all.

# CHAPTER FOUR
## *Shattered Hopes*

RAYNER'S SPIRITS REMAINED HIGH in the aftermath of the 1894 Populist defeat. Clearly the People's Party had gained ground. A sizable number of African Americans—although not yet a majority—had voted the Populist ticket. Total black voter turnout had approached 80 percent, and for the first time in a generation Texas Democrats polled a minority of all votes cast. Populist gains were especially dramatic in view of the fact that the Democrats had patched up the 1892 rift in their party, and the Republicans had once again fielded their own slate of candidates. The most pressing political reality facing Rayner and the Populists was obvious as they looked to 1896: if the votes of Republicans and other minor parties could all be combined under the Populist banner, the hated Democrats could be ousted.

In the politics of the 1890s, this required fusion. Texas Populists disagreed over the wisdom of marriages of convenience with other parties. Some pointed out that fusion had been used successfully at the local level and in legislative and congressional races. In this pragmatic view, defeating the Democrats justified fusion among Populists, Republicans, or Prohibitionists. Others took a more principled stance, preferring defeat over a potential dilution of the Populist platform.

National politics greatly complicated the issue of statewide fusion. The problem was this: to sanction a fusion between Populists and Republicans in Texas was to give tacit approval of comparable fusion agreements between Populists and Democrats in the northern and midwestern states, where the minority status of the Democratic Party resembled that of the Republicans in the South. If Populists in southern states could make deals with Republicans, and Populists in northern states make similar deals with Democrats, where would that leave the *national* Populist Party when it came time to choose its presidential ticket? Would some sort of fusion be attempted at the national level? If so, with what party, and with what consequences for Populism?

The likely answers to these questions disturbed Texas Populists. By 1895 many of them, including Rayner, were beginning to fear that northern Populists might try to strike a fusion deal with Democrats at the national level—an arrangement that would require the Populists to endorse a *Democratic* presidential ticket. This was a possibility because many Democrats had recently been converted to one minor Populist cause: taking the nation's monetary system off the gold standard and replacing it with a gold-and-silver, or bimetallic, standard. Southern Populists like Rayner understood that the coinage of silver would result in only a modest expansion of the nation's money supply. Only the full slate of Alliance/Populist demands—including the Subtreasury Plan—would bring the financial relief and the political reforms that farmers and laborers so desperately needed. But as Democrats at the national level warmed to the idea of endorsing the bimetallic standard, Populist-Democratic fusion became a more palatable alternative for Populists outside the South. In Texas the Populists' cry went up in 1895 and 1896 to "stay in the middle of the road," their slogan for remaining steadfast to the entire Populist reform program. The "middle of the road" slogan also carried with it the tremendously important idea that the People's Party had to be a *national* party rather than a sectional one. By staying in the middle of the road, Populists—especially black ones like Rayner—understood that the party would chart a middle course between the northern Republicans and southern Democrats. Only in this way could racial fears be pushed to the background and constructive government again become the focus of American politics.

No group in Texas was more distressed by the talk of fusion at the national level than were the black Populists. Rayner was unable to attend the hastily called February meeting of the state executive committee, but he wired his white hometown comrade E. S. Peters to act as his proxy with instructions to oppose any fusion deals with Democrats. When he learned that the committee had endorsed a recent statement by the national Populist committee chairman advocating an "honorable union of all the reform forces along those lines that will best promote the welfare of all our people" in the upcoming election, Rayner fired an angry letter to the Populist state newspaper. "What do you mean by 'along those lines that will best promote the welfare of all our people'?" he asked. Rayner was understandably suspicious. He theorized that supporters of silver coinage were "trying to erase the best part" of the Populist reform program. Undoubtedly dedicated to the midroad position in its entirety, Rayner clearly believed that to surrender the comprehensive reforms of Populism in favor of one minor issue, silver, was to surrender Populism itself. Worst of all, he knew that national Populist-Democratic fusion would largely end black participation in the third-party movement. Populists would no longer need black votes and the avowedly white-supremacist Democrats would gain control of Populism once and for all. For Rayner, staying in the middle of the road meant not just smart politics but perhaps the last chance African Americans would have to participate meaningfully in politics.

White Populists from all parts of the state concurred with Rayner in his alarm over possible Populist-Democratic fusion in the upcoming presidential contest. By April 1896 the pages of the Populist press bristled with warnings about the intentions of the national committee. "There is danger ahead," wrote N. A. Gann of Bud, Texas. "I do not like the utterances of our national chairman. I am afraid there is something wrong." H. C. Howell of Jasper knew exactly what was wrong. "That it is the purpose of [national Populist officials] to lead the Populist party, bag and baggage into the camp of the enemy at St. Louis on the 22d day of next July, is now perfectly plain," he explained. To Texas Populists like Howell, who had spent years battling the Democratic Party, the prospect of the upcoming national Populist convention nominating a Democrat was unbelievable. "Is it possible," he asked, "that they can succeed in carrying out their treasonable design?"

Texas Populists realized their worst fears when the Populist national convention met in July. Elected by local Populists to represent the Seventh Congressional District, Rayner numbered among the nearly 1,400 Populists who assembled in St. Louis, knowing that two weeks earlier the Democrats had nominated Nebraska's William Jennings Bryan, a fiery champion of silver coinage. To the horror of the Texas midroaders such as Rayner, a majority of the convention delegates supported the Populists' nomination of the Democrat Bryan. To no avail, the Texans led the fight against the Bryan nomination, with Rayner and every one of the state's 103 delegates opposing fusion to the bitter end. Dallas County's Populists reflected the attitude of the party's members in Texas. In the midst of the convention they sent their delegation this message: "Five hundred Populists say never surrender. Bryan means death."

The Texans, deeply embittered, returned home to a hero's welcome and were dubbed "the Immortal 103" for having stayed in the middle of the road. All spring long the political air in Texas had buzzed with rumors that Populist-Republican fusion at the *state* level might be consummated, for many Texas Populists would just as soon vote for the Republican presidential candidate, William McKinley, as for the Democrat Bryan. As early as March the *Austin Statesman* wrote about "a big political scheme" being hatched by Republicans and Populists. It reported that at the February meeting of the Populist state executive committee in Dallas "the Republicans made a proposition to the Populists looking to a fusion during the coming campaign that would be mutually beneficial to both parties." The proposed fusion would, in effect, trade Populist support for McKinley in return for Republican votes for the Populist *state* ticket. Leaders of both parties denied that such an agreement had been reached, but the rumors persisted.

While Rayner felt concerned about developments on both the state and national levels, he could not ignore his grassroots organizational work. Throughout 1895 he had traveled extensively in the eastern half of Texas making speeches, organizing black Populist clubs and helping to arrange the enormous camp meetings that had become a trademark of the third party. Ashby, the longtime chair of the state executive committee, aided Rayner in scheduling an uninterrupted speaking tour during July, August, and September. He appealed to "all patriotic Populists who can reasonably do so" to send a small donation to help defray the black committeeman's expenses. "The work I want Rayner to do," Ashby frankly explained, "no white man can do." Published schedules of the black orator's itinerary from the hot summer of 1895 testify to the grueling pace he set for himself. In a three-week period in late August and early September he spoke in twelve counties, almost certainly appearing numerous times in each one. At camp meetings he shared the spotlight with national Populist personalities such as Jacob S. Coxey, Charles Macune, and Cyclone Davis.

In the early months of 1896 Rayner showed no signs of relaxing his relentless crusade to spread the word of Populism among black Texans. Most politicians campaigned mainly in the summer and fall preceding elections, but not the orator from Calvert. Of course, the average white politician was also a planter, lawyer, or businessman, and campaigning took him away from his livelihood; Rayner subsisted on the proceeds from his speeches. One Democratic newspaper reporter commented on the way in which Rayner "converted his speech into silver at its conclusion." "He has evidently been a preacher," another reporter observed, "judging from his appeal for funds at the close of his argument. The collection was a decided success as was the speech, from a Populist's standpoint."

One can scarcely overstate Rayner's power as a public speaker. Twentieth-century Americans living in the age of microphones, amplifiers, and the electronic mass media will never be able to appreciate fully the degree to which nineteenth-century orators could mesmerize a crowd. Whites and blacks alike marveled at the forty-five-year-old Populist's power over an audience. In a letter to the *Southern Mercury*, a third-party partisan captured something of the flavor of an 1896 Rayner speech: "What crowds of people, what throngs of people, by fours, by dozens, on foot, on horses, in buggies, in wagons, above the roars of applause and clapping of hands, you hear the sweet music of the voice of the illustrious Rayner. Now like a wild tornado, now like a summer evening breeze, pointed, logical, severe, yet soft and gentle, the spirit of God is plainly mirrored from his heart, carrying conviction at every breath. God speed his good work!" When he spoke in towns and cities, Rayner invariably attracted listeners from both races. From the few surviving accounts of these speeches, it is possible to piece together the substance of his message as the party reached its greatest test, the 1896 elections. Employing the overblown rhetoric and pretentious vocabulary that characterized nineteenth-century political oratory, he would commence with a history lesson, Populist-style. According to Rayner, the United States was "a great country, a giant with his head [b]athing in the ice water of the Arctic ocean, his feet in the turbid waters of the gulf, his left hand on the golden gate and his right in the billows of the Atlantic." This giant would rise "with the might of a Hercules and stamp the pigmies"[sic]—the Republican and Democratic parties—"into the deep, sad mud of defeat and the deep damnation of retribution." "God put the Democratic party into the world to foster and protect slavery until the savage negro was civilized and Christianized," Rayner theorized. "That accomplished he put the Republican party in motion and built it up to free the negro." "The evolution of parties," he thundered, "must ever proceed." Like most other nineteenth-century Americans, Rayner subscribed to the idea of historical progress, but as a Populist he could not accept the contention that such progress was necessarily continuous and inevitable. His belief that freedom depended upon eternal vigilance and that corruption put the survival of the republic in jeopardy furnished him with the rhetorical weapons needed to attack the current state of southern politics. Thus near the end of a typical public appearance he proceeded to the audience's favorite part of the speech, the roasting of the Democratic Party:

> The Democratic drag has held back the South, and she is raising a lot of empty-headed and empty-pocketed ninny-heads to vote the same old time-worn ticket of the father and grand-pap. The country [is] not enjoying the summer excursions and champagne banquets nature provides, for the effluviant corpse of a mission-ended-wet-nurse-of-slavery party obstructs the open sesame to National and individual suc-

cess. The best elements of the grand old Republican and Democratic parties [are] volunteers to help the Populists clean out the old stables and bury the occupants so deep in mundane mixture that Gabriel will need subsequent assistance to produce power to wind his horn loud enough to call them to resurrection.

Rayner told his 1896 audiences that in the upcoming elections blacks were going to reverse their traditional loyalty to the Party of Lincoln and vote the People's ticket. Referring to the old parties' all-too-common practice of buying black votes, he contended that "a negro will gladly accept and chuckle over every dollar he can get from boodlers [bribers], but when he goes to the polls he will vote his own way." But Rayner also lectured the African Americans in his audiences about their shortcomings as voters. "There is a difference," he chided them, "between a negro and a white man: a white man votes from the head; he votes his mind; the negro votes from his heart; he is sentimental on the wrong ocassion [sic]." Rayner claimed that if a black voter "likes a white man he will even vote for a white Democrat solely because he likes him." Then he would turn specifically to the blacks in the crowd and pointedly remind them that "it will be a snowin' in h__l before a white Democrat votes for you because he likes you."

When he addressed his white listeners, Rayner underscored the absurdity of southern whites remaining Democrats solely "to keep down negro supremacy." "A Democrat," he told his audience, "goes to bed at night and dreams he sees a nigger with the courthouse on his back running off with it. The idea of 8,000,000 blacks, most of them ignorant and nearly all poor, gaining supremacy over 64,000,000 of intelligent whites. Do you white men here believe it?" He mounted a scathing attack on the corruption of the state and national Democratic administrations, reserving some especially pointed barbs for Governor Charles Culberson and Texas Democrats in Congress. He emphasized the role black voters had played in the election of past Democratic governors and predicted that his people would never again repeat their mistakes. Rayner closed with a reminder to blacks that their "only hope for justice" lay with the People's Party.

When he "came in like a storm" to deliver this speech at Market Square in Houston, white hecklers tried to disrupt his talk. The white newspaper reporter covering the speech went on to report that Rayner, undaunted, "aroused the crowd to numerous applauses by his quick-witted thrusts," telling the hecklers that they were "unmanly" in trying to keep him from exercising the privilege of free speech. That Rayner dared to castigate white hecklers in public bears witness to his courage, and the fact that he could get away with it suggests that white Populists were willing—at least on this occasion—to stand by their black ally. After his appearance a spectator told a reporter, "Houston has felt the storm and may take gracious comfort that a single house is left standing or that one lone official is left to tell the tale of political devastation."

Rayner's outspoken fearlessness in defending Populism and exposing Democratic corruption was also evident in a series of essays he wrote for the Populist press. One such piece appeared prominently on the front page of the *Southern Mercury* under the headline, "The Colored Brother. A Spicy Letter from J. B. Rayner." In it the black Populist spared no faction from biting criticism. The Lily-White Republicans, he explained, quit the regular party because the black race "sent too many incompetent and ignorant delegates to Republican conventions, thus making the deliberation in these conventions ridiculous." Rayner believed that with African Americans out of the picture the Lily-Whites would successfully "appeal to complexional prejudices, blue veins, straight hair, and business sentiments." But at least the Lily-Whites were sincere in their bigotry. In comparison, Rayner called the black Republicans under Cuney's leadership "sordid mercenaries in politics," and the few whites in the Cuney faction nothing but "the mephitic vaporings from a cadaverous carpet-bagism."

As hard as he was on Republicans, Rayner was even rougher on the Democrats. He likened President Grover Cleveland to Benedict Arnold for continuing to support the gold standard (a position Cleveland's own party was in the process of abandoning). But Rayner reserved his harshest invective for the silver (or reform) Democrats, led by William Jennings Bryan. Labeling them "chronic office-seekers" with "no political conscience or principle," he charged that they would "accept any platform to get a Democratic nomination, and then jeer and ignore it to get elected." Rayner believed that these Democrats were "Populists in faith, but are too cowardly to confess it." The sooner they went "to pluto's laboratory" [hell], the better it would be for the South. The black Populist knowingly predicted that the so-called reformers in the Democratic Party would write a confusing platform filled with "platitudes and ambiguous terms," and in the next election they would "use bribes, deception and shotgun intimidation to capture negro votes." Time would prove him entirely right in this regard. "The only rights we negroes will ever enjoy," he concluded, "will be the rights the southern white man gives us." The only whites in Texas who were prepared to grant those rights were Populists. "Vote the People's Party ticket," Rayner instructed his readers. "We will get better wages for our work and we will have better times in the south."

Rayner's writings in the Populist press in 1896 also displayed a growing class consciousness on his part. In April he penned an editorial chronicling the rise of the reform Democrats in Texas. Rayner explained how ex-governor James Hogg had ridden his towering ambition into the governor's office. The "piney wood's parvenu," as Rayner sarcastically called Hogg, had won the governorship by cynically playing the farmers against the railroads. The real problem, then, as Rayner diagnosed it, did not lie in a Marxian conflict between labor and capital; America had grown undemocratic because the government had erected unnatural barriers and brought unnecessary antagonism between the classes. Although they supported public ownership of the railroads, Populists like Rayner generally did not question the sanctity of private property. Indeed, they were motivated largely by the fact that small landowners were rapidly *losing* their land and being driven into a condition of dependency that no amount of hard work would ever allow them to escape. Populists criticized a government that granted special privileges to large corporations like railroads, enabling capitalists to exploit the average farmer or mechanic. In Jim Hogg, Rayner saw the corrupt professional politician that the Founding Fathers had warned against. Hogg, according to Rayner, represented the interests of neither capital nor labor; he had simply taken advantage of the farmers' resentment of the railroads to win the governorship, and then his much-ballyhooed Railroad Commission had done little to curb the railroads' abuses. "Down this dismal sewer, with his true character hid from an expectant people, he walked into the gubernatorial office," wrote a disgusted Rayner.

Explaining the current political partisanship and class hostilities, Rayner argued that in normal times the American people would not be politically divided along class lines. However, "the greed, rottenness and incivism of the two old parties" had disturbed the natural state of American politics and had divided citizens into two antagonistic classes. The lower class (or "plebians" [sic] as Rayner called them) supported the Populist cause. The upper class ("patricians") clung to the two old parties and were "secretly together on all vital issues." Rayner then conducted the type of analysis of the upper class that might lead the casual observer to see a Marxist flavor in his words. He accused the old parties of having an alliance with organized religion, the mainstream press, and "all the bankers and corporations of the world." But to Rayner neither capitalism nor wealth were inherently evil. He criticized the Democrats and the Republicans not so much because they were in league with capitalists but because of the ways in which the leaders of the corrupt major parties had perverted the proper economic relationships in America, pitting one economic group against another. In order "to carry out their fiendishness," Rayner suggested, "the two old parties . . . will make the banker intimidate the merchant and manufacturer, and the merchant will intimidate the small farmer, and the farmer will bribe or intimidate the laborer and tenant farmer." Put in these terms, no single economic class was innately bad; the blame lay with the political forces that caused one group to exploit the other. Professional officeholders like Jim Hogg lacked the necessary civic virtue to represent the organic interests of all the people. When faced with promoting their own personal interests or those of the American people, such politicians always chose the selfish route.

Since the Republican and Democratic bosses had ceased to represent anyone's interests other than their own, Rayner predicted that in the upcoming elections the old parties would undoubtedly avoid real issues. Men fighting for office rather than principles would choose instead to harp on the danger to white supremacy and make emotional appeals to party loyalty. In Rayner's words, the moral bankruptcy of the Republicans and Democrats would thus force them to "ignore civilized warfare, and . . . do only bush fighting." Rayner optimistically predicted that the old parties' "dishonorable methods" would fail to save them, "for the leaven of the People's Party has permeated all the people, except the incorrigible." In this analysis "all the people" included the businessman, planter, yeoman farmer, and manufacturer, as well as the sharecropper and laborer. It also would have to include blacks as well as whites.

With Rayner and other midroad Populists holding such views, one can readily see why they would have serious reservations about fusion on the level of statewide elections with either of the major parties. To combine with either one was to join forces with the enemy. In precinct and county races it was a different case, mainly because fusion at the local level between Republicans and Populists had proven successful not only in bringing victory at the polls but also in securing greater justice for blacks. A few third-party countywide officeholders such as sheriffs Garrett Scott of Grimes County and A. J. Spradley of Nacogdoches County seemed remarkably dedicated to protecting the lives and property of their African American constituents. When Rayner, by his own account, "broke up the Democracy" in Nacogdoches, he felt it worth public mention that "not an unkind word was said" to him while in the county. He considered the Populist lawman Spradley "brave as a lion" and pronounced him "the best sheriff in Texas." But a fusion agreement at the *state* level went beyond mere pragmatism. To many it seemed to involve a real sacrifice of principle, and that could backfire at the polls; a formal alliance with either the Democrats or the Republicans could alienate thousands of dedicated Populists. Any formal statewide fusion arrangement would be extremely risky.

In late summer 1896 Rayner and the other leaders of the People's Party in Texas began to focus their attention on the upcoming state elections. Texas Populists held their state convention in Galveston two weeks after the national People's Party fused with the Democrats in St. Louis. During the short time between the two meetings, renewed talk of a deal between Populists and Republicans at the state level reached a fever pitch. The Populists continued officially to deny any such intentions, but their anger at their party's actions in St. Louis, combined with their unceasing animosity to the Texas Democratic Party, lent credence to the fusion talk. On the eve of the state convention, influential Populist editor Milton Park of the *Southern Mercury* angrily wrote that there was "no possibility of the People[']s party of the south fusing with any other party" but then qualified the statement, saying that the Populists "might join forces with . . . the Republican, Prohibition or Union Labor party, but never with the Democratic party." "That sort of a fusion is too disgusting to be thought of."

In reality, Rayner and the more radical leaders of the party had already determined that a fusion between Texas Populists and Republicans was a necessity. All political eyes in Texas were focused on Galveston as the first of nearly 2,000 delegates began assembling for the state convention on August 4. Rayner was among the first to arrive, probably to engage in some very private discussions with Cuney and several other Republican leaders, all of whom conveniently appeared in Galveston the day before the Populists' convention began.

The ensuing convention was a stormy affair. Nominating a state ticket proved uncontroversial; with the death of the beloved Nugent, labor attorney Jerome Kearby of Dallas—a proven friend of the working man—had become the consensus choice for governor. The real fight revolved around the issue of fusion at the state level. Everyone had his own opinion and believed it represented the genuine midroad position, but the truth was plain: the middle of the road had already been forsaken at St. Louis.

Nevertheless, as far as John B. Rayner was concerned, there was never any question about the necessity of repudiating the national convention's nomination of Bryan. On the second day of the Galveston meeting, thirty-five black delegates responded to Rayner's call for a caucus in order to "find out where they stand." Although they did not know it at the time, it would be another sixty years before African Americans would again have the ability to play this sort of political role in major party politics in Texas.

Rayner closed the session both to whites and to the press but allowed one white *Dallas Morning News* reporter whom the blacks trusted to attend the conference. The delegates sensed that they had arrived at a crucial moment not only in the life of their party but in the long struggle for black rights in Texas. Their discussions, recorded in detail by the lone reporter, capture the mixed feelings of optimism and anxiety shared by the black Populists.

Rayner called the meeting to order with a blunt statement of fact: "The Democratic party can not be trusted with the finances of the country and they can not be trusted with the rights of the negroes." Rayner then turned the meeting over to L. N. Sublett of McLennan County, leaving at least one of the delegates confused. Nelson Polleyman of Caldwell immediately complained "that the negroes had been advised not to support W. J. Bryan for president, but Rayner had left them right there without telling them who they should vote for." Of course, no one seriously believed that Rayner was finished. "We'll reach that soon," Sublett replied knowingly.

Some informal discussion followed, with the blacks seemingly no more united on a course of action than their white counterparts. One thing, however, was clear: the black Populists found any fusion deal with Republicans extremely distasteful. Exerting his independence, a delegate from Columbus argued that "J. B. Rayner has been my political orator for four years, but he can't lead me into anything I don't know all about. . . . I take the position that even if Bryan is a stanch Democrat and I can get a part of what I want I will do it and wait for the rest. We must act carefully and not on an impulse." At this point Rayner quietly defended his position: "There has been no talk of any Republican [fusion] or of any vote. All I ask of you is not to vote for a Democrat."

A short discussion followed, whereupon Rayner introduced a series of resolutions he had written for consideration by the African

American delegates. After endorsing the full range of traditional Populist demands and correctly dismissing silver (the bimetallic standard) as a Democratic "panacea," the resolutions addressed the real issue at hand, fusion. Both major parties were "evils," Rayner's document stated, but of the two, the country had "more power to endure" McKinley than Bryan. Thus the critical resolution stated that if the Populist national committee would not repudiate Bryan, then "we will lead our state with the name of William McKinley and the Republican state electors and we will give the state to McKinley if the Texas Republicans will vote for [Populist Gubernatorial nominee] J. C. Kearby."

The chair allotted each delegate five minutes to state his views on Rayner's resolutions, and again the delegates debated earnestly. One argued that the Republicans could not be trusted to uphold their end of a fusion bargain. Another hoped the resolutions would be voted down, saying, "If the negro is to be used as a purchasable commodity, no wonder the white people have no confidence in him and no use for him."

But other delegates supported Rayner's position. As one argued, "If you don't adopt this resolution my county is going Democratic. This resolution is what we need." Another concurred, saying, "I left the Republican party and joined the Populist party because I believed that the Populist party is the one for the negroes. I canvassed my county before I came here, and if the Populists stick to the Democratic nominee, there are many there who are not going to vote for him. I don't say, mind you, that I'm going to vote for McKinley, but never will I vote for Bryan." This last Populist concluded his remarks by suggesting that he might sit out the presidential election rather than vote for Bryan *or* McKinley.

Now Rayner felt that things were getting out of control. He chastised his fellow delegates: "I called you here for consultation, and it's not treating me right that there should be such insinuations that I have tried to lead you astray—that I am trying to sell you to the enemy." Rayner's "hurt feelings" elicited cries of "No, no; nothing of the kind meant." So he continued. "What my object in this is I will tell you plainly: I want the negro Populists to get together and agree, that we may show that we do not intend to support any Democrat; so that fact may be very apparent."

Thereafter the tide of the caucus shifted in Rayner's favor. The closing arguments of two more delegates revealed their understanding of the political realities facing black Texans at the climax of the Populist revolt. The first delegate asked, "When I go out to make a speech in this campaign the first thing that is going to be thrown at me is that the Populist party has indorsed [sic] the Democrats [at the national level]. And how am I going to answer them?" The second replied, saying, "We are tired of Democratic supremacy and tyranny, and we can't get rid of it by voting for and electing Bryan . . . Of two evils choose the lesser—and at this time McKinley is the lesser. . . . We are here to do something, ought to do something, so let's do it."

Rayner's resolutions passed, eighteen to thirteen. The divided vote illustrates the terrible quandary that the black midroaders faced. Like their white counterparts, these black Populists were disgusted over the proposed deal with Texas Republicans, but Bryan was even more unacceptable. They understood that their dream of a national party that would include African Americans and speak to their interests was in dire danger. Their party's nomination of Bryan had eliminated the middle-of-the-road position. But despite the defeat of Populist principles on the national level, the black delegates could take some comfort in the idea that maybe the Democrats were finally to be defeated in Texas. With this goal in mind, they were not afraid to go on record as supporting fusion with the Republicans on a national level. Most of them understood that there was still something very important at stake.

The convention did not follow Rayner's lead in *openly* endorsing a political trade with the Republicans, but behind the scenes the groundwork was laid for exactly such a deal. With the support of party leaders, including Rayner, a three-man campaign committee was appointed to meet with the Republicans and work out the details of fusion. Officially the Populists endorsed neither Bryan nor McKinley, but it was clear that Texas Republicans would support the Populist state ticket in return for Populist votes for McKinley. It would be up to state and local Populist leaders to make sure that the rank-and-file went along with the plan on election day.

The convention ran into an unplanned fourth day, due to lengthy speechmaking and parliamentary maneuvers. By Saturday morning only about 150 delegates remained convened, but they still had to elect a new state executive committee and adopt a platform. The executive committee, as usual, was chosen by congressional districts and consisted of thirteen white men. When the time came to elect the two delegates at-large, Rayner and two whites received nomination. Rayner said he would prefer to withdraw from the race, deferring to the two white nominees, but he expressed concern that his absence from the committee would lead Democrats to say, "'Oh, yes, since the Pops have gotten to the point where they can elect a ticket they deny the negro any representation.'" Rayner's supporters would not allow him to withdraw. The chair told him he was out of order to try, and the election proceeded. Early votes favored Rayner and were divided between the two white candidates. When one of the white nominees withdrew, the delegates elected Rayner by acclamation.

The 1896 platform differed little from the 1894 document. One new feature was a plank declaring the party to be "in favor of equal justice and protection under the law to all citizens without reference to race, color or nationality." This was a significant statement, but the platform committee had balked at a resolution that would have recognized the black citizen "in such positions as his capacity fits him to fill." This veiled reference to black officeholding proved too much for the white Populists. Once again, the Populists had traveled further toward racial equality than had either of the major parties, but still they had gone only part of the way. Sadly, it was about as close to equality as southern blacks would come for the next sixty years.

Rayner and the Populists left Galveston and commenced one of the most bitter and violent campaigns in Texas history. As planned, the Texas Republican convention placed no state ticket in the field, thus indicating their acceptance of the fusion plan. The Populists' main task—in addition to the usual efforts to win converts to Populism—was to convince Populist voters to support the fusion deal. Although the Populists continued to deny that any formal agreement had been struck to swap Populist presidential votes for Republican gubernatorial votes, the Democrats missed no opportunity to lambaste the Populists for their alliance with the mostly black Republicans. Rayner and the black Populists, of course, had no such qualms, nor did the bulk of the adamantly anti-Bryan white Populists. But the Democrats' charges of racial treason and their appeals to white solidarity were difficult for many white Populists to ignore.

As the campaign progressed and the fusion plan became more widely known, white Populists from across the state registered their refusal to support McKinley. One reportedly said that "if the Republican electors are put on the populist ticket I will not vote for them nor any candidate who is a party to such a fusion." Some Populist candidates for local offices withdrew rather than join "one of the most unholy political coalitions ever conceived by the mind of man. . . ." The words "unholy," "disgraceful," "dishonorable," and "unseemly" pepper the white Populist utterances from this period. Such was the opposition of white southerners to the idea of uniting with the party of "Radical Reconstruction" and "Negro domination."

No Populist struggled harder to lay to rest potentially destructive racial tensions than Rayner. Arguably, no Populist leader had more at stake. His December 1895 editorial in the *Southern Mercury* had opened with the explanation, "I am glad the time has come when the monster breath demagogues will have to quit talking about 'social equality,' 'negro supremacy' and the 'solid south.'" The black Populist dismissed these terms as "slang phrases" left over from Reconstruction, terms that had no significance in the 1890s. Throughout the campaign of 1896 Rayner used this same line of reasoning on the stump. In September he made his standard stump speech in Cherokee County. The Democratic *Houston Post* reported that "his discourse, from beginning to end, consisted of a frantic appeal to the colored voters to vote the Populist ticket in the hope of securing social equality." The black orator allegedly held out the "tempting bait" of black participation on juries in the event of a Populist victory, and he "was interrupted at frequent intervals by the cheers of white Populists present." Of course, Rayner never advocated social equality any more than did white Populists, but for the Democratic correspondent covering the speech, the black Populist's advocacy of African Americans serving on juries implied just that. In the eyes of the reporter, the white Populists' cheers of Rayner's speech branded them as traitors to white supremacy.

In addition to their charges of racial treason against white Populists, the Democrats also tried to deceive the black voters. The Populist state platform provided that "each race shall have its own pro rata proportion of the school fund," meaning that the black and white public schools should receive equal per capita funding. The Democrats issued propaganda across the state informing blacks that the plank meant that they would receive an unfair portion of the fund. This was demagoguery at its worst, because under Democratic rule most African American schools had never received more than a fraction of the funding that white schools did. By comparison, the Populist planks on black education had been among the party's most liberal and just racial pronouncements.

Democrats scored a major coup a month before the election when one of the state's leading black Republicans, William M. "Gooseneck Bill" McDonald, bolted the fusion arrangement and threw his support to Democratic gubernatorial candidate Charles Culberson. McDonald would later become one of the richest African Americans in the nation through his astute business, fraternal, and political activities. The Populists charged that the Democrats had bribed McDonald, but this accusation was never proven. He actively campaigned for the Democratic state ticket, and his defection caused serious damage to the fusion cause among black Republicans.

Finally, Democrats did not fail to invoke another time-honored racial tradition in the South, physical intimidation. On the eve of the election, L. N. Sublett, who had chaired the black Populist caucus at the Galveston convention, spoke at Willis, Texas. After his speech, a mob gathered at the home of the local black family with whom Sublett was staying and demanded that the family surrender their guest. A lynching appeared imminent, but "the conservative element" in the mob overruled it. Instead, the mob forced Sublett to leave the county

"on foot, with his grip in one hand and his overcoat on his arm."
Shots were fired as he hurriedly left, but Sublett escaped unharmed.
Local Democrats later justified their actions, claiming Sublett had
used "violent and incendiary" language in his speech when he called
"the entire [Democratic] party a set of ___ ___ ___, an epithet too
vile to print."

Rayner continued to campaign with unabating vigor. The week
after the state convention, Dallas Populists invited him to join Kearby
and other party heavyweights for a grand rally in the North Texas
city. Rayner was unable to attend, but at the conclusion of the event
Judge E. L. Wood read a statement from the black leader. "I am sorry
I can not attend your ratification meeting on the 22d instant," the
letter read, "but if our Savior continues my life, I and 65,000 other
negroes will be at J. C. Kearby's ratification meeting in November
next, at which time Texas at large will ratify the action of our state
convention." Rayner predicted that Texans would elect Kearby governor "because he is a friend to right, justice and the common people"
and because "we want our state capitol to be the temple of justice
and charity, and not an Augean stable,* to house a lot of political
vampires." Rayner promised to keep "speaking and making converts
for Populism and votes to help elect my ideal man, the Hon. J. C.
Kearby." With that, the rally adjourned.

Rayner worked furiously until the election. As soon as the
Galveston convention adjourned in August, he had taken the first
train back to Calvert to confer with Robertson County's Populists.
At that meeting Rayner told his hometown allies that 85 percent of
the county's blacks would vote the Populist ticket. Robertson County
Democrats followed the actions of Rayner and the Populists with
intense interest. African Americans had held offices in the county
since Reconstruction, and the Democrats had not carried the entire
county in thirty years. As the Populists, Republicans, and Democrats
held their local nominating conventions, the *Houston Post* correspondent in Robertson County described the intensity of the situation: "county politics is almost a white heat now." Little was being
said about the national races; all eyes were focused on local affairs.

*From Greek mythology, a place of corruption or filth.

By the end of August, partisans in Robertson County were formulating their campaign strategies. On August 30, the *Galveston News* published a report from Calvert announcing that "J. B. Rayner, the Populist leader in this county, will be a candidate for the legislature." The *News* failed to elaborate on the report, except to say that "Rayner is well educated, a fluent speaker and a shrewd political wire worker, and will be hard to beat." Nothing more was ever said about Rayner's alleged candidacy. The story may have been nothing but a rumor, or perhaps Rayner discovered that his name had been suggested for office and quickly put a halt to the talk. At any rate, in mid-September the county's Populists met in convention and immediately appointed a committee to confer with the local Republicans. After two days of negotiations the two parties agreed on a joint county ticket in which four of the nominees were Populists and the balance Republicans. Several of the fusion candidates were black, including Jesse Smith for county commissioner from the Calvert precinct, and the longtime Republican leader, Alex Asberry, for state representative.

The Democrats soon announced their ticket as well. Among their number was O. D. Cannon, the incumbent Democratic county judge. Cannon was something of a legend in Robertson County. First elected county judge in 1890, he enjoyed a well-deserved reputation as a violent character. By 1896 he already had killed three men. In the most celebrated incident, a black lawyer, Hal Geiger, who had served a term in the state legislature as a Republican, was arguing a case in Cannon's court. A witness recalled years later that Geiger made an insolent remark and was promptly corrected by the judge. When Geiger "refused to show the judge the proper respect," Cannon calmly raised his revolver and put five bullets into the lawyer. In this case, as in the other two murders Cannon committed, the jury refused to convict the hot-tempered judge. Presumably, black insolence justified homicide in Robertson County. When he was not standing trial for murder, Cannon was finding other ways to flaunt the law. The county's district court records are sprinkled with cases of gambling and other minor offenses involving Cannon not as county judge but as defendant. Earlier in 1896 he had been tried (and cleared) on extortion charges when he allegedly took payoffs to dismiss certain cases.

Cannon and like-minded Democrats had begun to despair of ever putting an end to black officeholding in Robertson County. As an old-timer recalled years later, "the conservative white voters were beginning to realize that severe measures would have to be taken to assure the election of [only] white people to office." On election day they put those measures into motion. The county seat, Franklin, was crowded with armed men all day. Democrats "quietly deposed" the black town marshal before the polls opened, and forty men with Winchester rifles stationed themselves at the county courthouse to turn away all but Democratic voters. In the lower end of the county, a large company of African American voters was marching from their homes in the Brazos bottoms, accompanied by a brass band, to cast their votes in Hearne. An armed delegation of Democratic horsemen accosted them on the Little Brazos River bridge, throwing the band instruments into the river and dispersing the crowd. At Hearne, "a great number of pistol shots were fired in front of the polls when the negroes . . . came in to vote," and subsequently the box polled 600 fewer votes than in the previous election. In one rural precinct that traditionally gave the fusion ticket a ninety-vote majority, the presiding officer reported that "a masked man took the box and returns away from him." In another the Democratic candidates for sheriff and tax collector stood at the door of the polling place, one with a gun and the other with a club, and held off black voters. About mid-afternoon word reached Judge Cannon that in spite of these county-wide efforts the election might hinge on his home precinct. "I went down to the polls and took my six-shooter," he recalled. "I stayed there until the polls closed. Not a negro voted. After that they didn't any more in Robertson County." Cannon boasted that he personally stood off 1,000 African Americans that day. When asked many years later about his violent role in bringing white rule back to the county, he explained that "I only shot when I thought I had to. I know God pulled me through."

In spite of these extreme measures, the election was very close. Initial returns gave the black fusion candidate for state representative, Alex Asberry, a sixty-five vote majority out of nearly 5,000 votes cast. When election officials blatantly counted him out, Asberry made the mistake of threatening to contest the election. Cannon confronted him in a Franklin saloon and shot the black politician in the arm. Asberry then fled on foot for Calvert, ten miles away. Democrats put the county bloodhounds on his trail, and tradition in Robertson County holds that the wounded Asberry beat the hounds back to Calvert. Only Jesse Smith, the black candidate for county commissioner, won a victory so clear-cut that it could not be stolen. He quietly declined to accept the office, and his Democratic opponent was duly sworn in. Thus white supremacy returned to Robertson County.

The Populist defeat in Rayner's home county was reflected in the statewide results. Amid great excitement and widespread fraud, intimidation, and violence, the Populist gubernatorial candidate, Jerome C. Kearby, lost to Democrat Charles Culberson by a vote of 298,528 to 238,692, and the Democratic presidential ticket carried the state with 54 percent of all votes cast. Populist or fusion congressional candidates ran strong races in five districts but won none of them. The radical Populist leadership's high hopes for statewide victory were shattered, and the fault rested largely with the Populists themselves. Fusion had failed. Analysis of the election indicates that over 40,000 of those who had supported the Populists in 1894 returned to the Democratic Party—enough defections to cost Kearby the election. Estimates of African American voting reveal that the votes were almost evenly divided between Culberson and Kearby. While this was enough to indicate the considerable success of Rayner's efforts, it also underscores the effectiveness of the Democrats in controlling the black vote.

In the end, the politics of race had proven fatal to the Populist cause in Texas. Too few blacks had been willing to abandon the Republican Party and embrace Populism, leading the Populist leadership—including Rayner—to adopt the desperate tactic of trading Populist presidential votes for Republican gubernatorial votes. But if the Populist leadership was willing to enter into such a deal with black Republicans, the Populist rank-and-file was not. Democratic race-baiting was successful in persuading thousands of wavering Populists that the Democratic Party was the only guarantor of white supremacy. In later years, Rayner would come to understand this with great clarity, and it would embitter him toward poor whites for the rest of his life.

Back in Robertson County, E. S. Peters sold his Populist newspaper in Calvert and gave up on politics for a number of years. In a spiteful mood, the county's Democrats voted to prohibit anyone who had voted for the fusion ticket in 1896 from participating in future Democratic primaries. Rayner may or may not have returned from his last campaign appearance in time to witness the violent overthrow of Populism in his home county; he may well have been at the head of the company of blacks who were terrorized on the Little Brazos River Bridge en route to vote. The lack of surviving information on his whereabouts on that day comes as no surprise, for in subsequent years he understandably kept very quiet about the election of 1896. For the next two years, as one Populist editor put it, the People's Party of Texas "drifted with no firm hand upon the helm." When the state convention met in July 1898, black delegates were "conspicuously absent." Various accounts in the state press of executive committee meetings fail to mention Rayner's name, and the papers took no notice of whether he won reelection to his place on the committee or appeared at the state convention at all.

Yet amazingly, he returned to the campaign trail in one final, futile effort to salvage some vestige of independent politics in Texas. In July 1898 Rayner announced that he would be holding "colored People's party campmeetings" during the next two months if local Populists would help him with the arrangements. "This is the time for action, and there is no place in human endeavor for the idle and lukewarm," he trumpeted in the pages of the *Southern Mercury*. A week later his spirits remained high as he anticipated another campaign: "Past defeat has not discouraged me; I am again ready for the onset." In August Rayner announced one of the most extensive speaking tours of his career, a punishing twenty-four-stop canvass of the south-central Texas Black Belt. Gone, however, were the days of statewide campaigning in every East Texas county, converting blacks to Populism and trying to bring local Republican and People's parties into agreement on a fusion ticket. His call for aid in holding black camp meetings apparently went largely unanswered, and Rayner ultimately directed his efforts toward the lone congressional candidate in the state whom he thought might stand some chance of defeating a Democrat. The campaign would provide a poignant postscript to Rayner's years as a Populist.

The contest pitted one of the rising stars of Texas politics against a grizzled veteran. The young Albert Sidney Burleson was a prototype of the new "progressive" southern Democrat. With the backing and assistance of the wily political manager Edward M. House, Burleson was conducting his first congressional race, promising to support adoption of a state income tax, denouncing imperialism, and speaking harsh words against monopolies. No one needed to point out that he also stood for white supremacy. George Washington "Wash" Jones opposed him in the contest. Jones was truly one of the unique personalities in the history of Texas politics. A unionist before the Civil War, the Bastrop native had served as a colonel in the Confederate Army and won the lieutenant-governorship in 1866 under Presidential Reconstruction. He soon renounced his allegiance to the Democratic Party and embarked upon a quixotic thirty-year career as the leading independent politician in the state. Endorsed at various times in his long career by Republicans, Greenbackers, Independents, Union Laborites, and Populists, the awkward, folksy, and sincere Jones won election to Congress in 1878 and 1880 and lost two consecutive races for the governorship in 1882 and 1884. So politically independent was Jones that he refused even to affiliate formally with the People's Party, though he held Populist views and the party endorsed him. He had always sought black votes, and black Texans genuinely respected him. A decade earlier, in the aftermath of the 1887 prohibition campaign, a Waco newspaper editor had written that those seeking to defeat the Democratic Party in the future would "enjoy the embraces" of both Rayner and Jones. Now, at the very end of the Populist era, that prediction could not have been more accurate.

Following a two-week campaign swing in September that took him through eight of the district's nine counties, Rayner returned to Jones's home county, Bastrop, to spend the last days of the race marshaling black support for the independent candidate. A local newspaper reported that Jones was "standing up well in a hopeless race for congress" and expressed surprise "that a man of his age could endure the fatigue of a campaign against a young and brilliant man like Albert Burleson." Rayner met with his usual success on the stump, and even the Democratic press reported that a speech he made in Jones's behalf was "witty and at times almost eloquent." When the returns came in, however, it was apparent that the young Democrat had buried the old crusader. Jones carried only his home county of Bastrop, where a devoted personal following gave him a lopsided two-to-one margin. By contrast, in Washington County—with one of the largest black populations in the state—the Independent ticket polled only 724 votes to the Democrats' 5,296. The day had passed when a black majority in a Texas county spelled trouble for Democrats. Burleson was to serve eight successive terms in the House of Representatives, followed by eight years as postmaster general. In one of his first acts in Woodrow Wilson's cabinet, he put into motion a plan that helped to accelerate the segregation of federal government offices and facilities. With Burleson on his way to national fame, Wash Jones accepted defeat for the final time, and John B. Rayner's career in insurgent politics came to a dreary end.

# CHAPTER FIVE

# Feeding the Wolf

THROUGHOUT HISTORY, dissenters who have tried to reform repressive political systems have often faced long years of exile when their efforts to change their societies failed. Such was the fate of John B. Rayner at the dawn of the twentieth century. He had not left Texas or the nation, but he was in exile just the same. The events of the late 1890s not only dealt a mortal blow to southern dissent as personified by the People's Party but effectively ended Rayner's participation in politics. His reform movement utterly destroyed and his people terrorized, the once-proud orator and party organizer disappeared almost completely from the public view for four years.

The magnitude of the Populist defeat can be gauged by the tenor of public affairs in and around Robertson County. The Populists in Rayner's home county had been so demoralized by the violent events of 1896 that the party's candidates two years later would neither accept nomination nor campaign. "This is as it should be," noted a local Democratic editor. "The white people of the county should stay together from this [point] on and forever do away with the colored politician." The week after the election, a Democratic newspaper in Calvert rejoiced that "The last nail was driven in the coffin of Robertson county Populism last Tuesday." The white people of the county were "at last of one mind, politically speaking," and were finally united in favor of "white supremacy and good county government economically administered." "Today the white people are in the saddle," explained the editor of the *Calvert Chronicle,* "and they are determined to stay that way."

In nearby Grimes County, Populism met with a later, but equally dramatic, demise. The Populist-Republican coalition there had succeeded in electing a number of county officials, including a black county clerk and a white sheriff, Garrett Scott, who employed black deputies. With the coalition firmly in control, supported by the county's blacks and poor whites, the People's Party managed to survive intact until 1900. Perhaps inspired by the example of Robertson County, Democrats in Grimes formed a White Man's Union that systematically harassed and terrified Populists of both races. The political confrontation culminated in the assassination of the black district clerk and a five-day siege by the White Man's Union of the county jail, in which the sheriff and his deputies were barricaded. The critically wounded sheriff, Garrett Scott, relinquished his office and retired from Populism when state troops arrived to escort him from the county.

In less dramatic fashion, old Populist leaders one by one said their good-byes to the party. For most of them, however, it meant more than just a change of occupation. Rayner's friend A. J. Spradley, the Nacogdoches sheriff who had courageously defended blacks from the lynch mob, released his farewell statement to the press. Rayner had called Spradley "the best sheriff in Texas," and the Populist lawman had become famous throughout the state. Communicating something of the spirit that, at its best, Populism had embodied, Spradley wrote that he was relinquishing the sheriff's office "for life." Addressing his notice to "those who have been my friends, white or black, rich or poor, and to those who have been otherwise," the defeated sheriff could only take comfort in "the satisfaction of knowing that I have tried to do my duty." Spradley and some other Populists eventually drifted back to the Democratic Party, justifying it on the grounds that the Democrats had endorsed many of the third party's demands. Compromise, they believed, was better than surrender. Even these Populists, however, felt ambivalent about their return to the Democracy. Joe Eagle, the young, dashing, former Populist congressional candidate from the Houston district, regretted the party's defeat but could "see no good to come from keeping up the populist party organization." "I prefer, right or wrong, to fight in the open," he wrote. "I am not ashamed of the part I have played—it has, I hope, been open and manly."

By the turn of the century the party lay in such shambles that even prominent Populists often did not know where their erstwhile colleagues stood politically. In July 1900, Populists in the northeast Texas town of Paris tried to organize a party camp meeting for the following month. The chairman of the encampment committee, well-known third-party man James W. Biard, drew up a list of speakers to be invited to the gathering. His list included Jerome C. Kearby, Joe Eagle, Stump Ashby, and John B. Rayner. Kearby, his health rapidly fading after years spent pursuing losing causes, had retired from public life and would be dead in a few years. The youthful Eagle had announced his return to the Democratic Party three weeks earlier. Rayner's friend Ashby, who had refused a Democratic bribe to withdraw from the lieutenant governor's race in 1896 and who had spent most of his personal savings in the Populist cause, wrote Biard a frank private letter declining the invitation. Ashby's letter, like those of Spradley and Eagle, captures the strong emotions felt by the old Populists in the wake of the party's defeat: "I will say in reply to the invitation of your committee that I have spent the best years of my life in defence of the people, as I believed it. I did it largely at my own expence. Now I am old & poor, and I cannot leave my only hope of a livelihood—that is work on my farm, & go out to make speeches for my expences I am sorry that I am not younger & in better financial condition, so that I might again go out on the free list, but I *cannot*."

There is no record that Rayner ever replied to the committee's invitation. If he had answered, the response likely would have echoed that of Ashby, for Rayner had also spent the best years of his life in defense of the people, as he believed it. There was, however, one major difference; while Ashby was poor and disillusioned, he was white. Biard was asking Rayner to come to one of the most rabidly antiblack sections of the state to speak on the virtues of biracial cooperation. Paris was the same town in which several years earlier a black man accused of a crime had been brutally tortured with a hot poker before being burned alive before thousands of white onlookers. Under the circumstances, it is not surprising that Rayner chose not to accept the invitation.

Indeed, Rayner not only had dropped from the political scene, but he even abandoned his home in Calvert at times during these years. As if addressing Rayner personally, a Robertson County editor in 1900 asked, "Pop[ulist], where art thou? Art thou asleep or gone visiting? I never hear from you. . . . If you don't show up I don't know what will become of Mr. Negro." Rayner had gone to Victoria, Texas, 150 miles to the south of Calvert. He had secured a part-time pastorate with a church in the South Texas city and, although his home and family remained in Calvert, he spent much time preaching in Victoria. It is, in fact, the only record that survives of Rayner ever actually being formally identified with a congregation. Perhaps he had to remove himself far from his home region—where the people had not so often heard him denounce "worthless and characterless" black preachers—in order to find a church that would have him. It is not known how long Rayner maintained this long-distance affiliation, but during his long years of exile from public affairs it provided not only means of subsistence for Rayner and his family, but it also served as a safe harbor from the smoldering racial and political animosities of Robertson County.

Rayner no doubt needed the extra income during the first years of the new century, for he suffered a serious financial and emotional setback in 1901. The *Southern Mercury* reported on April 18 that Rayner's home in Calvert had been nearly destroyed by a fire that damaged his kitchen and household furniture. Losses were estimated at $600, an enormous amount for a man of his meager means. Reminding the paper's readers that Rayner was "an old-time middle of the road Populist," *Mercury* editor Milton Park requested that "the old Populists who know personally of his faithfulness to the Populist party, would do well to remember him in a substantial way now in his loss." Whether any assistance materialized is not known, but given the poverty of so many Populists, the contributions could not have been great.

Although the events of the late 1890s had seemingly made it clear that Populism was dead and that Rayner's place in politics would be severely circumscribed in the future, it was not easy for him to cut all ties to his beloved cause. In 1902 a small group of old midroad Populists who refused to countenance surrender attempted a reorganization of the state and national parties, along with socialists and other reform groups, under the new name of the Allied People's Party. Milton Park led the movement in Texas and Jo A. Parker of Louisville, Kentucky, became the chairman of the national executive committee. In the Spring of 1902 Parker put out a call for "one thousand true men to work for the National Committee at reasonable compensation." These so-called "national organizers" presumably would be given authority to organize Allied People's Party clubs, and the compensation would probably be a percentage of the membership dues. Breaking a public silence that had lasted nearly four years, Rayner wrote to Parker in May, offering his services, to which Parker quickly assented. The *Mercury* applauded Rayner's commission, commenting that "the people of his race . . . above all people, should be eager to free themselves from the imperialism of combined capital." In his letter to Parker, Rayner proudly proclaimed that his "fervor [for] Populism grows with my age," and that he was "getting ready for the coming political onset." He reminded the *Mercury*'s readers that he needed financial support if he was to "write, and speak and work" for the movement. But he claimed that he was "in the discussion and agitation to stay until the people will think wisely and act righteously." His name began to appear in the paper on lists of available Populist speakers.

The *Mercury* soon reported that Rayner was renewing his efforts to spread the word of Populism among blacks and was even planning to travel to Houston County to speak and organize Populist clubs. In August Rayner published the schedule of a proposed eleven-stop speaking tour through Henderson, Anderson, Leon, Madison, Montgomery, and Burleson counties. However, the campaign never began. The Allied People's Party did not survive for long, and it was unrealistic to expect that either blacks or whites in East Texas would have lent any assistance to Rayner's efforts to recruit black voters for the party. To have followed through with his campaign plans would not only have proven futile but probably dangerous.

While Rayner faded from the public memory, the triumphant white Democrats of Texas moved to consolidate their power and finalize the subjugation of their black countrymen. Throughout the Populist revolt, voter turnout among black Texans had steadily risen, reaching a high of 85 percent in the presidential election of 1896. By the fall 1902 elections, African American turnout had fallen to a pitiful 23 percent through a combination of fraud, intimidation, terror, rules barring blacks from voting in local primary elections, and a general demoralization of black voters. That same year the state legislature submitted a poll-tax amendment to the voters of Texas. The measure, which did not affect the 1902 general elections, passed easily with 65 percent of the vote. The voters had simply written into law and given permanence to what in reality had already been accomplished: the disfranchisement of most blacks, along with many of the poor whites who had cooperated with them in the Populist revolt.

Although Democrats led the movement for the poll tax, it would be a mistake to blame them exclusively for disfranchisement. White Populists also contributed significantly to the passage of the poll tax. The *Southern Mercury*'s Milton Park blamed the victims, suggesting that blacks were "miserably to be blamed to let the Democrats use them in such a way." Park advised blacks to "learn from experience, and develop their manliness" so that the Democratic "rascals cannot handle them in that way." The Populist spokesman then issued an ominous—and prophetic—warning: "If the negro does not qualify himself to be a freeman, and act like one, the American people will become so thoroughly disgusted with this sort of thing after a while, that they may rise in their might and take the ballot away from him. Therefore, let the negro consider and be forewarned." Thus when voters went to the polls in 1902 to decide the poll-tax issue, most blacks stayed at home, but twice as many white ex-Populists supported the poll tax as opposed it. Rayner fully realized that large numbers of his former white Populist allies had voted for the measure that would help curtail black participation in politics.

A month after the voters approved the poll tax, Rayner wrote an editorial that seemed to signal a new direction in his political thought. Published in the *Houston Post* and reprinted by the *Southern Mercury,* the essay—astonishingly—endorsed the poll tax. The new amendment, according to Rayner, "virtually eliminates the worthless negro from politics and the ballot box; but its adoption will not disfranchise the negro who respects his citizenship, but will awaken to patriotic activity every negro in Texas whose spark of manhood is still alive." Whatever he may have thought about the poll tax before its adoption, there was no advantage to be gained by opposing it after the fact.

However expedient it may have been, Rayner's decision to endorse the tax was not entirely inconsistent with his long-held beliefs. Throughout the 1890s he had been critical of blacks who had voted Democratic, and of the thousands of others who had sold their votes or who refused to vote other than a straight Republican ticket. For years he had been telling his fellow blacks that a black man "has to have some sense before he can become a populist." Therefore, after the downfall of Populism, Rayner was critical of the role that he believed blacks had indirectly played in causing their own disfranchisement.

Rayner's endorsement of the poll tax must be viewed in light of the fact that he blamed both poor blacks and poor whites for the defeat of Populism. "The great number of ignorant and mercenary voters among my people has compelled white people in the South to resort to the white man's primary and the white man's union," he wrote in 1904. Like his father before him, he subscribed to the principles of Revolutionary-Era republicanism, which held that virtue and intelligence were essential in political participation. For more than a decade he had battled against poor blacks' stubborn attachment to the Republican Party, and he had seen their votes corrupted by Democratic liquor and money. Likewise, he could not have so soon forgotten how many poor whites had responded favorably to the racial demagoguery of the Democrats, helping them put down the Populist experiment in biracial politics. If restricting suffrage to those possessing the resources to pay a poll tax would eliminate the corrupt or ignorant voters of both races, so much the better. As a black southerner in the early twentieth century, Rayner felt no constraints in criticizing the conduct of his fellow African Americans; he opened fire on everyone whom he believed had prevented the realization of a republic governed by virtuous black and white citizens.

Rayner's indictment of ignorant voters forms a central theme of his writings on disfranchisement in the years after 1900. "The South acted wise and patriotic when it required the black voter to prepare himself to vote," he wrote in a characteristic statement. He frequently argued that "as long as ignorance goes to the ballot box imbeciles will go to our legislative halls." Although he believed that "all men have worth and hold fee simple* title to justice," Rayner firmly held to the conviction that "there is no place in a democracy for the ignorant and immoral." The poll tax, if fairly administered, would restrict suffrage to those taxpaying citizens of both races who held steady jobs and fixed residences in a community; if it disfranchised many blacks, it would do the same to many poor whites. Rayner may have supported the poll tax in 1902 hoping to forestall a statewide white primary and stop the spread of the countywide white primary. Perhaps by this show of good faith, white Texans eventually would restore suffrage to worthy blacks in those counties where they had lost it. The poll tax may have been harsh medicine, but it was more palatable than the alternatives.

Rayner's endorsement of the poll tax makes him sound like Booker T. Washington, the famous black Alabama educator who counseled African Americans to work hard, get a practical education, and "accommodate" themselves to white supremacy. However, Rayner's acceptance of the poll tax must be compared to his harsh condemnation of the other principal means of disfranchisment, the whites-only primary. The ex-Populist pulled no punches in attacking the white primary, for it was a disfranchising method that discriminated solely on the basis of skin color, without regard to education, character, property ownership, taxpaying, or any of the standards that might be used to measure a citizen's worthiness to vote. In Rayner's logic,

*without restriction

the white primary accomplished the opposite goal of the poll tax; it gave the ignorant and vicious members of the white race the ability to govern the intelligent and virtuous representatives of the black race.

Rayner's bitterness toward the white primary is evident throughout his political essays of the post-Populist period. If the South had "acted wise and patriotic" in restricting the suffrage of ignorant blacks, he wrote, it "acted otherwise when it failed to require all white men to do the same." He harshly criticized the "ignorant poor white men in the Democratic party in the South, who dominate the white man's primaries," citing their ignorance "of the mission of republics and democracies." He repeatedly argued that "intelligence and virtue are the only certificates that can give a right to vote," and he stated flatly that "the color of a man's epidermis is no prima facie evidence of political competency or incompetency." "There is no relief in politics," explained a frustrated Rayner, "as long as the white man's primary names the officers who are to be elected to preserve the peace and dignity of the state, and if there was no white man's primary there would be no relief as long as the majority of the negro voters did not comprehend the import of their votes."

Rayner's attitudes toward suffrage furnish one of the keys to understanding his public course after 1903. As his positions on the poll tax and white primary demonstrate, that course embodied a confusing and often inconsistent mix of accommodation and militancy. Even throughout the Populist Era, Rayner had understood that the realities of the turn-of-the-century South required that even a black activist like himself defer to white leadership; Rayner's Populist stump rhetoric had always contained an acknowledgment that the white people of the South were the "Negro's best friend." But following the traumatic events of the late 1890s and early 1900s, accommodationist rhetoric and actions assumed a far more prominent role in Rayner's public life. It galled him, but he could see no alternative.

For Rayner, living in the changed atmosphere of Texas politics in the early 1900s, one overriding goal assumed precedence over all other considerations. That goal was securing some recognition, however small or symbolic, that *all* African Americans were not inherently and permanently inferior to all whites and that therefore certain blacks deserved a meaningful voice in government. It was obviously a greatly diminished goal compared to the high hopes of the Populist period. "My class of Negroes," he contended in a very Jeffersonian tone, "have race love and race pride and are very ambitious to form among ourselves an aristocracy of virtue and esthetical and industrial intelligence." He was now willing to sacrifice the votes of the majority of blacks, if only the tiny class of educated, property-owning, taxpaying Negroes would be allowed to participate in politics on an equal basis with whites. On one hand, that meant endorsing poll taxes, literacy tests (for screening voters), voter registration rules, property requirements, or any other restrictions as long they were to be applied equally to blacks and whites. On the other hand, it meant fighting the white primary and other forms of strictly racial discrimination, including extralegal forms of physical intimidation. Rayner was prepared to acquiesce to white leadership as long as some qualified class of blacks could freely and independently participate in the selection of those leaders. The experiences of the Populist revolt had proven the folly of hoping that all black adult males would be allowed this right, or that they would exercise it intelligently and honorably. The stuffed ballot boxes, bartered votes, gunplay, demagoguery, and sheer ignorance of the voters in the 1890s not only had contributed to the undoing of Populism, but it had led to a racist backlash on the part of whites unparalleled since the darkest days of Reconstruction. This backlash convinced Rayner that participation in Populism, however noble its intentions or pregnant with democratic possibilities, had been a tragic mistake for blacks. Populism had promised all black men meaningful suffrage, but its defeat had rendered it infinitely harder for even the most intelligent and virtuous blacks to achieve political equality.

Securing truly free voting rights, if only for a handful of the most worthy African American citizens, became one of the chief motivating factors in the last fourteen years of Rayner's life. Until intelligent and virtuous blacks could cast a ballot unimpeded and uninfluenced by white laws, violence, or chicanery, the entire race would be denied the simple promises of life, liberty, and the pursuit of happiness set forth in the Declaration of Independence. The elaborate economic reforms so central to Populism seemed rather esoteric and visionary compared to what had become the cold reality of the twentieth century: most blacks could not go to the polls on election day and vote. It was now clear to Rayner that Populism had been a gamble with much higher stakes than he had imagined, and the price of defeat was enormous. By moving too fast to secure the sweeping reforms of Populism, blacks had lost whatever political gains they had made since the end of Reconstruction. They would have to start over. If "bad white men" had destroyed Populism, as Rayner believed, it was because they were successful in "exploiting the credulity of my ignorant race."

With the political opportunities for African Americans so diminished, Rayner turned to education. He long had worked for the betterment of black public education in Texas. As a member of the committee that framed the Populist state platform, he had been instrumental in drafting provisions calling for an equitable division of the state's public school funds and for African Americans' control of their own schools. He also had frequently criticized the quality of the state's black schoolteachers and advocated better training and higher standards for those who would educate black children.

Rayner's first recorded public statements after his five-year exile from public life focused on the current state of public education. Writing to the *Houston Post* in May 1904, the former Populist began his essay entitled "Solution of Negro Problem" by praising the generosity of the white man. In an accomodationist tone reminiscent of Booker T. Washington, Rayner stated that "the South is the best place on earth for the negro, and the Southerner is the negro's best friend." This friendship existed because "the Southerner is taxing himself to help educate the negro." Rayner's words painted a picture that most white southerners would have applauded. He commended the South's generosity in employing black laborers, in helping blacks with their church work, and in knowing "how much length to give the political tether which is to hold the negro until his citizenship is superior to his ambition." Having paid lip service to white supremacy, he then got down to specifics. "It is the duty of the State to educate the negro to do the work which the business interests of his country will call on him to do," he declared. "The negro needs a moral education rather than a book education, for the negro's sense of gratitude has no memory in it, and his conscience needs culture. The Southerner in his effort to solve the negro problem is making some sad mistakes." Those mistakes, according to Rayner, lay not in the fact of tax-supported public education but rather in the way the common schools were being managed. He identified poorly qualified teachers and an inappropriate curriculum as the chief sources of trouble. Fearing that the legislature might soon act on current proposals to eliminate all public funding for black schools, Rayner offered a startling alternative: "I would close all the negro free schools in Texas for two years."

Rayner went on to explain his proposal. Closing the schools for two years would enable blacks to rid their schools of corrupt, incompetent teachers who were "sucking the moral strength from the negro race." It would also "cure the school-teaching mania, now an epidemic among the young negroes." The hiatus in state-supported education would force "the best negroes" to "quickly organize themselves into independent school communities and employ only the best teachers, and thus draw the line between the good negro home and the bad negro home, and this will help the good negroes to become more self-dependent and independent, and the good negroes would soon build up among themselves an aristocracy of virtue and intelligence." During the two years that the schools were to be closed, the state government was to "keep separate and intact the unused money belonging to the negro schools, and at the end of the two years apportion the money to the use and benefit of the negro schools." Rayner's proposal essentially would privatize black education. It also would remove the schools from white control, a goal that the Populists had supported. At the same time, however, the plan would preserve some public funding for black education.

Nobody paid any attention to Rayner's proposal, but his new role as educational theorist apparently opened a door of opportunity for him in late 1904. The previous year a black educator, Dr. James

Johnson, had laid the plans for a Negro "normal and industrial" college to be located at Conroe, about forty miles north of Houston. The school was to be modeled on Booker T. Washington's Tuskegee Institute, which stressed practical vocational training for blacks. As the plans for the new school began to take shape, Johnson realized that the success of a private black college would require someone with extraordinary ability in fundraising, a skill that he apparently did not possess. Toward this end, in October 1904 the school's board appointed Rayner its financial agent.

Conroe College had modest beginnings, but there was cause for guarded optimism over its chances for success. When Rayner became its financial agent, the institution owned eight acres of donated land, one four-story building with twenty-three rooms, two smaller buildings, and enough lumber for the construction of another "commodious" building. In the 1904 fall term the school boasted forty boarding students and about one hundred others. Perhaps even more important for an enterprise of this sort, the school enjoyed the formal blessing of local white leaders. Several of Conroe's leading citizens, including a banker, a judge, and the city's mayor, sat on the school's advisory board. In an era when some whites were criticizing the very idea of educating black people, it would be vital for the institution to have the dominant race's stamp of approval.

It would take more than nods of approval, however, for a new black college to survive. Conroe College needed money. Tuition and contributions from the state's poverty-stricken blacks would never amount to more than a fraction of the required funds. State aid was a possibility, but a remote one in the current atmosphere of distrust and resentment between the races. Church-supported colleges could draw upon the collective resources of whatever convention or association they were affiliated with, but Conroe College was to be secular. Therefore, the new school's only chance of survival lay in Rayner's ability to tap potential sources of white philanthropy. This method had worked for Booker T. Washington at Tuskegee; maybe it could work at Conroe.

The new financial agent wasted no time in unveiling his scheme to raise money. If Populism had taught Rayner anything about conducting a successful crusade, it had taught him the importance of publicity. For the next two-and-a-half years, Rayner kept Conroe College almost constantly in the press, filling the columns of both the large urban dailies and small country weeklies with glowing reports of how the school was helping to solve the race problem in Texas. The goals of the institution were identical to those he had recommended for the state's public school system. "Scholars" at Conroe College were to be taught:

1. The science and art of politeness.
2. How to obey law and respect for public sentiment.
3. How to resist temptation and be virtuous.
4. That idleness is sin—all labor is honorable.
5. That a good character is the greatest wealth.
6. That the white people in the South are the negro's best friends.
7. That Christianity means love and service.

Two weeks after his appointment to the fundraising post, Rayner began to publicize his most ambitious project at the school. He proposed that the white people of Texas donate money for a large, four-story, fireproof brick building dedicated "to the memory of the faithfulness of the slaves to their masters' families during the war between the States from 1861 to 1865." The building would be dubbed the "Hall of Faithfulness," over the main entrance of which would hang an appropriate commemorative marker. Rayner in no way equivocated as to his goals for the college. "This school must be made to Texas what Tuskegee is to Alabama."

Although this accommodationist approach was markedly different from his old Populist militancy, Rayner's appointment to the Conroe post allowed him once again to engage in the kinds of activities that he had long relished: travel, speechmaking, and agitation. Besides the long-term objective of raising money to erect the Hall of Faithfulness, the school needed an immediate $2,000 to repair existing buildings and complete campus projects already underway. He immediately took to the road, crisscrossing the eastern half of Texas and cultivating his old Populist contacts in both the black and white communities. In January 1905, D. C. Tharp, a Conroe bank president who sat on the college's Advisory Board, assured Rayner that "the board has full confidence in you." Tharp informed his black associate that "the School is rapidly becoming a state more than a local institution" and reminded Rayner that blacks as well as whites would have to be forthcoming with their support. By late March, Johnson and the white board had rewarded their financial agent with the additional title of president of the college. It is doubtful that the bestowal of this honor actually involved any change in Rayner's status as chief fundraiser. Johnson's official title became Secretary and Founder, and he appears to have continued as chief administrator of the school. However, the title of president gave Rayner additional status in his high-profile mission of publicizing the institution and soliciting donations. The white press was soon describing him somewhat inaccurately as "the moving spirit in the school" and calling him "the Booker T. Washington of Texas."

Rayner's efforts on behalf of Conroe College placed him in some unusual situations. If politics makes strange bedfellows, raising money for the Conroe Normal and Industrial College made even stranger ones. In April 1905 Rayner traveled to Palestine, Texas, and appeared before the reunion of the John H. Reagan Camp of the United Confederate Veterans. The old Rebels were impressed with Rayner and passed a resolution endorsing the Hall of Faithfulness. Rayner later repeated this performance at the annual national meeting of the Confederate Veterans in New Orleans. He clearly understood the strong emotional attachment that white southerners felt for the Lost Cause, which by the early 1900s had achieved the status of a secular religion in the South. The former Populist appeared ready to assume any posture—no matter how humiliating—in order to raise funds for his new cause.

Rayner's work promoting the school among Democratic politicians also created some strange bedfellows. The same month that the former slave appeared before the Confederate veterans in Palestine, Rayner paid a visit to Alexander Watkins Terrell. The seventy-five-year-old Terrell had been an officer in the Confederate Army, U.S. Minister to Turkey, and a leader of the state Democratic Party for forty years. He introduced the first poll-tax measure in the Texas legislature in 1879 and had been one of the state's leading proponents of suffrage restriction ever since. Firm in his belief that "the foremost man of all the world is the Anglo-Saxon American white man," Terrell sponsored legislation in 1903 and 1905 that brought sweeping reforms in Texas election laws. As a leader of the progressive wing of the Democratic Party, he had done as much as any man in the state to disfranchise blacks. It is no small irony, therefore, that Terrell sponsored a resolution in the state House of Representatives endorsing Rayner's efforts to build the Hall of Faithfulness at Conroe College. Resolutions and letters of endorsement from state senators, supreme court justices, and members of the railroad commission soon followed. But as in the case of the Confederate veterans, resolutions and praise alone did not pay teachers' salaries or fund the construction of campus buildings. If Conroe was indeed to become the Tuskegee of Texas and John B. Rayner its Booker T. Washington, applause and resolutions had to be backed by cash. Although he must have been disappointed that donations failed to keep pace with public displays of approval, Rayner knew from the first that his school's prosperity would depend largely on his success in cultivating white philanthropists. And from the start he cultivated them with a vengeance.

Whatever his contemporaries may have thought of Rayner, nobody could accuse him of timidity. If one sought money from rich white Texans, he reasoned, what better place to begin than with one of the richest white men in the state? Exactly one week after being appointed Financial Agent of Conroe College, Rayner addressed a letter to Houston businessman John Henry Kirby. Thus began a remarkable relationship between an often-reactionary white millionaire capitalist and a black former agrarian radical that continued for the rest of Rayner's life.

In his best handwriting, Rayner addressed Kirby: "Sir: I beg you to forgive me for intruding upon your valuable time. I do so, because I believe you to be greatly interested in all endeavors for human amelioration." In a blatant refutation of Populist doctrine, Rayner explained that he believed "the rich people of every country, to be the custodians of the people's happiness. " Assuming the most accommodating stance possible, Rayner made his pitch for Kirby's aid:

The altruistic and unrequited work which I am now doing for human amelioration, would be greatly emphasized, and made more effective, if you will condescend to acquaint yourself with the purposes and work of the Conroe-Porter Industrial College, at Conroe, Texas. I am the financial agent for this school, and if the Lord will permit me, I shall go North among your millionaire associates next Spring, and try to raise some money for the school, and before I start, I shall ask you for a recommendation, and in the interim, I beg you to con[de]scend to inquire about the school, and see if it has merits and purposes which you can approve. . . . I do hope that all true chivalrous patricians like yourself, will take some interest in this school and help make its work more effective.

Yours in much humility,
and for Human Amelioration,
J. B. Rayner.

Rayner had played his cards well, for the wealthy Houstonian was immediately receptive to the idea and took a sincere interest in the work being done at Conroe.

At the turn of the century, Kirby was a classic American success story. Rising from modest beginnings to become the unrivaled king of the East Texas lumber industry, he later expanded into railroads and oil. As a believer in Andrew Carnegie's Gospel of Wealth philosophy, whereby the wealthy had a duty to help society by contributing to worthy causes, Kirby cultivated a reputation as a philanthropist and model employer. During hard times, however, he responded to labor unrest by suspending paychecks, blacklisting, and hiring strikebreakers. And unfortunately for Rayner, he had caught his potential benefactor at a bad time. The "Prince of the Pines"recently had overextended himself through some complex oil dealings, and his main endeavor, the Kirby Lumber Company, had suffered in the process. Payrolls went unpaid, millworkers walked off the job, and by early 1904 Kirby's lumber and oil companies were both placed in receivership. He was by no means broke, but the next five years were difficult for him.

In light of his dire financial situation as of December 1904, it is all the more surprising that Kirby took an interest in the black supplicant from Conroe. Yet Kirby not only replied promptly and positively to Rayner's initial request for letters of introduction, but he invited his new acquaintance to Houston, expressing a wish "to confer with you personally before hand as I think I can make some suggestions that may be of value to you." Throughout the remainder of Rayner's association with Conroe College, the two men corresponded frequently, with the black fundraiser asking the white tycoon's aid in obtaining letters of recommendation, securing appointments to speak to white business groups, and determining the best strategies for promoting the school. Kirby loved flattery, an art at which Rayner was well practiced. "I know your powerful influence in the social, commercial, financial, and political world," Rayner told Kirby, "and I know that your public spirited, broad[,] liberal, and resourceful mind . . . can evolve some effect[ive] plan, which will give me the ear of Houston, and I beg for it." Rayner knew, of course, that Kirby's avowed paternalism toward African Americans in no way made him any less a white supremacist. In a typical statement designed to appeal to his patron's racism, Rayner wrote, "I know that I have more respect and reverence for Southern taste, Southern customs, and Southern sentiment, and Southern traditions, than Booker T. Washington has, and I am no obsequious sycophant; but I am man and philosopher enough, to honor and reverence those racial esthetics, of the superior race, which centuries of thought, energy, patriotism, education, and religion have established immovable and indestructable in this country, for the immaculate preservation of the superiority of the Anglo-Saxon race."

Rayner's careful courting of Kirby finally bore fruit, though doubtless not as richly as the black leader had hoped. The Houston businessman ultimately contributed $250 to Conroe College. That sum, while hardly great, was nevertheless a considerable help to the cash-strapped institution. And considering the donor's seriously embattled finances at the time, it stands as testimony to Kirby's sense of paternalism toward blacks. Of course it also appealed to his personal vanity and soothed a conscience that may or may not have been bothered by the low wages and poor conditions endured by both black and white laborers in the Kirby mill towns. It might also pay dividends later, by promoting his reputation as a friend to African Americans, who might in turn serve as convenient scabs in some future strike. Whatever the personal motives of either man, the relationship between Rayner and Kirby says much about the state of race relations in early twentieth-century Texas. Kirby, an ultraconservative on most political issues, represented the opposite end of the political spectrum from Populism. He not only believed the People's Party to have championed "heresies in questions of policy and no principle," but he had even opposed William Jennings Bryan as a dangerous liberal. However, Democratic progressivism was the wave of the political future in the South, and progressive Democrats now supported many of the more moderate Populist demands. Yet those same progressives were at the same time the unrivaled champions of the most severe forms of racism. Rayner faced a cruel dilemma. He could support the progressives and their harsh brand of white supremacy, or he could join forces with conservative-but-paternalistic white southerners who stood for monopoly, the gold standard, political cronyism, laissez-faire government, and antiprohibition. White Populists could easily make their peace with the progressive Democrats, but when Rayner reentered public life in 1904, he made the only choice he could make. If blacks had any remaining allies among whites, those were the reactionaries, not the progressives. They were men like John Henry Kirby. It comes as no surprise, then, that in the hundreds of surviving essays, editorials, and letters Rayner wrote during the last fourteen years of his life, the word *Populism* never once appears. The reformers were now the enemy, and if John B. Rayner hoped to survive among the reactionaries, he had to try to forget that the Populist revolt had ever happened.

It is difficult to assess Rayner's overall ability as a fundraiser for Conroe College, for the glowing reports in the press undoubtedly give an exaggerated picture of his success. Still the school made major progress under the ex-Populist. By March 1906, near the end of Rayner's tenure at Conroe, the college was reported to be "in a flourishing condition." The number of boarding students had grown to 320, and Rayner believed that the school could easily have an enrollment of 2,500 were facilities available. He and Johnson employed a Tuskegee graduate to head the agricultural department, and student carpenters were productively occupied building a house. Equally encouraging reports came from the home economics department, where young women were learning the fundamentals of cooking, sewing, and managing a household. In early 1907 a number of important Texas business and political leaders were listed as contributors to the school, including George W. Brackenridge and Otto Wahrmund of San Antonio, George W. Littlefield and Edward M. House of Austin; and John H. Kirby, Samuel F. Carter, and James A. Baker, Jr., of Houston.

The most notable achievement came in late 1906, when Rayner secured $100 cash and a $1,000 loan to purchase about 100 acres of land adjacent to the school. The benefactor was Bertrand Adoue, a prominent banker and commission merchant of Galveston. A French immigrant, Adoue had gotten his start in New Orleans and for a while had settled in Calvert, where Rayner had made his acquaintance. The addition of the land—assuming the loan could be repaid—would enable Conroe College to conduct real agricultural training and at the same time raise a cash crop to defray expenses. In a letter to Rayner, Adoue proffered his best wishes for the school's success, along with some stern advice: "I hope that your proteges will appreciate what is being done for them by assisting you to liquidate the debt. They must be made to understand they are 'men,' and not 'wards.' As men, they will command the respect and even the admiration of the white race; as wards, they must be objects of contempt, and should not expect anything else." Relatively few white Texans in 1906 were willing to admit that blacks might "command the respect and even the admiration of the white race." Adoue was one of them; Kirby was another. Neither had much respect for the progressive wing of the Democratic Party. And as a wealthy banker and merchant, Adoue—like Kirby—represented most of the things that Populists had once despised.

Adoue also occupied a high position in the ranks of the Texas antiprohibition forces. Liquor had become an increasingly important and divisive issue in the state ever since the Democratic Party had succeeded in crushing the Populist revolt and "reforming" the electoral process. Many of the politicians who had first taken sides on the issue in 1887 were still in the fight twenty years later, trying either to banish alcohol from the state or to preserve Texans' right to imbibe whatever they pleased. Although Rayner had been in the thick of the 1887 prohibition campaign, stumping the state to enumerate the evils of strong drink, when the "wets" and the "drys" renewed their contest in the early twentieth century, John B. Rayner found himself on the opposite side of the political fence. In prohibition, as in so many other things, Rayner was forced to reckon with the new reality of the twentieth century. And the reality was that reformers—in this case the prohibitionists—were the faction most dedicated to the segregation and disfranchisement of black people.

While it may at first glance seem a contradictory twist, there were practical reasons, having little to do with racial liberalism, why the antiprohibition forces of Texas now recruited Rayner to speak on their behalf. The poll tax effectively had disfranchised a majority of blacks, but those who paid the tax could still officially vote. The white primary in most East Texas counties barred blacks from voting in the Democratic primary, which normally was the only election that mattered. But prohibition elections were different, because they were decided in the general elections rather than through party primaries. Furthermore, prohibition was an issue upon which whites often were fairly evenly divided. Therefore, much as they had during Populism, African Americans could again serve as a "swing" vote, at least in those counties with a significant black population. The opponents of prohibition thus found natural allies among blacks.

Like working men and women in other places and times, many black Texans in the early twentieth century enjoyed a good drink. Under normal conditions, a majority of them probably would eagerly go to the polls to fight prohibition. But the early 1900s were not normal times. The wets rapidly were realizing that it would take extraordinary efforts to induce blacks to pay their poll taxes and go to the polls in prohibition elections. Hard times continued to take their toll on blacks' pocketbooks, and fraud, intimidation, and plain disillusionment discouraged even those African Americans who could afford to pay the poll tax from exercising their right to vote. If the wet forces were to keep Texas from eventually going bone-dry, they would have to find ways to induce blacks to pay their poll taxes and cast ballots on election day to defeat prohibition.

During the years of Rayner's retirement from public life, the drys had been organizing. The Texas Local Option Association was founded in 1903 to encourage precincts, towns, or counties to ban alcohol. Soon, other antiliquor organizations, such as the Women's Christian Temperance Union and the Anti-Saloon League, stepped up the prohibition agitation. To counter the growing dry sentiment, the liquor industry created an organization of its own, the Texas Brewers' Association. The Association provided the structure for a cartel of the state's major beer breweries, led by St. Louis–based Anheuser-Busch. Over the next decade the Association fixed prices, divided territories among breweries to eliminate competition, and spent hundreds of thousands of dollars combating prohibition in Texas. The brewers had fought a losing battle against the adoption of the poll tax in 1902, and beginning in 1905 they employed Rayner to get out the black vote in local-option elections across the state.

Rayner plunged into the prohibition wars with his typical energy and dedication. If, as a former prohibitionist, he entertained doubts about the rectitude of the wet cause, the surviving historical record does not communicate those misgivings. For seven years beginning in 1905, the old Populist kept in almost constant contact with representatives of the Texas Brewers' Association, individual brewery officials, and representatives of local antiprohibition organizations, ready on short notice to travel to the scene of the next local-option contest. During 1905–1907 he kept a grueling schedule reminiscent of the Populist campaigns, splitting his time between his fundraising activities for Conroe College and campaigning against prohibition. The tactics were also similar to those used in the 1890s. Rayner typically would travel to a county in which a local-option election had been called and meet with leaders of the county or precinct anti-prohibition forces. He then would seek out leaders in the African American community, drawing on the huge network of acquaintances he had made during the Populist years for support in the new cause. Finally, he would arrange to make a series of speeches—often midnight rallies in backwoods black settlements—trying once again to conjure the oratorical magic of the past. No one could have been better suited to the purposes of the Brewers' Association in Texas.

Rayner's arrangement with the Association was an informal one; he was never a salaried employee of the cartel. Other than expecting the brewers to pay his expenses, he allowed them to pay him whatever they deemed him worth in a given situation. Part of this strategy no doubt stemmed from the need for a black to avoid appearing "uppity." Part of it may have been merely a wise ploy on his part to make his employers feel beholden to him rather than vice versa. However, much of his reasoning behind the arrangement came from Rayner's own scruples about being perceived as a hireling. After spending years as a Populist answering charges that blacks in the third party were nothing more than tools of ambitious white men, and after making precisely the same charge against blacks who voted Democratic, he could hardly justify his actions on grounds other than disinterested patriotism. He gained a reputation among many antiprohibition leaders as a man who was "patriotic enough not to make any specific charges." "I am satisfied," wrote another wet official, "that Mr. Rayner will do our cause a world of good! He is intelligent, has great weight with his people, and is not a 'paid' anti, but one from principle and at heart!" Patriotic or not, Rayner felt strongly compelled to work against prohibition. The chief goal of the wets was to persuade blacks to pay their poll taxes and then vote against prohibition. And since prohibition was closely identified with the progressive Democrats, it was natural for Rayner to oppose it. But at the practical level, antiprohibition held even more fundamental significance for Rayner: it simply kept blacks involved in politics. Almost any movement intent upon registering black voters and getting them to the polls would have gained Rayner's endorsement. Virtually any group—even monopolistic beermakers—would have constituted acceptable allies in the struggle to preserve black voting rights.

Correspondence of the Brewers' Association provides a fascinating glimpse into the inner recesses of early twentieth-century black politics. Apart from the considerable light that these records shed on the local-option fights, they also offer a more detailed examination of the kinds of techniques that Rayner no doubt used in the Populist Era. A 1907 local-option election in Travis County illustrates many of these techniques. In February Rayner wrote to brewers' representative Otto Wahrmund of San Antonio, apprising him of the probability that an election would soon be called in the county. The black politician had been to the county, and he warned Wahrmund that an election was coming. "I was in Austin last week," Rayner reported, "and while there I unearthed the purposes and plans of the pro[hibitionist]s." He went on to explain that the prohibitionists had already raised $3,000 cash for the campaign. Soon they would circulate the petition needed to call an election. Rayner told the brewer that as soon as the election was approved, the drys were planning to conduct a house-to-house campaign in the black community, employing women to spread literature. The money was to be used to print prohibition literature and pay black speakers. "If I had the money I would meet you in Austin," Rayner offered, "and we could do some effective work, and overthrow the purpose, and thwart the plans of the pros."

Six weeks passed, and the wets had done nothing. Rayner again wrote Wahrmund, cautioning the brewers to "prepare for a battle in Travis County." At that point Rayner asked his associate point blank, "Do you want me to manage the colored vote in that county during the coming campaign?" Always the optimist in the midst of an election, he assured Wahrmund that he had "full charge of the colored vote" in Travis County. Often this sort of request was all it took for the brewers to dispatch their black organizer to a county, but this time the brewery officials thought Rayner was mistaken about the strength of dry sentiment in Travis County.

On the verge of being left out of the campaign entirely, Rayner wrote to Wahrmund yet again. "I know the conditions in Travis County well, and I tell you now if the anti campaign is not wisely managed our side will suffer loss. I want to help win the victory in Travis. Again, let me warn you that danger is ahead, and we must not blunder." Rayner promised that if the brewers would finance his activities in Austin, he would "find out all the plans of the pros and make some speeches, [and] silence all the negro preachers" who had enlisted in the prohibition cause. By this time it was becoming apparent that Rayner had been right about prohibitionist strength in Travis County. A third brewery official, R. L. Autrey of the Houston Ice and Brewing Company, suggested to Wahrmund that he reconsider sending the black organizer. Autrey reminded Wahrmund that Rayner not only was the "manager of a negro college at Conroe" but that he was "a particular friend of the president of the negro college at Austin. I think he can truly close the negro church doors to the prohibitionists in Austin," wrote Autrey. Wahrmund finally acknowledged that what his fellow brewer said was accurate. "I know from personal experience that all you say of the gentleman referred to is only too true," he admitted, "and I am confident that he could help out a whole lot." He promised to recommend Rayner to the local antiprohibition committee in Austin.

As the Travis County campaign unfolded, it became clear that the drys were indeed well organized. On May 8 local antiprohibition chairman George W. Littlefield reported that the capital city was seriously divided on the question and that it would be "a hard fight." By the fourteenth, Rayner was "on the ground at work." He found to his dismay that the wets had done nothing at all to court the black vote. In contrast, the colored prohibitionists were "shelling the woods." The brewers gave him $50 to commence the campaign, and soon Rayner had "used that money and created a confusion and fight among the colored prohibition leaders," which enabled him to "take the zeal and rabid fanaticism out of the leaders of the colored pro campaign committee." He wisely did not elaborate in writing exactly what that meant. The black leader and his white counterpart quickly devised a satisfactory working arrangement. Littlefield furnished Rayner with "a full supply of refreshments," which the black manager used to open his campaign headquarters. Soon he had the black vote in line, and when election day came the wets carried Travis County by a comfortable margin.

In the county-by-county prohibition wars of the early twentieth century, as in the Populist campaigns, Rayner constantly had to harass his white political associates for adequate compensation. Although they almost always acknowledged his invaluable contribution to their cause, few antiprohibitionists were as honest as Rayner's friend Bertrand Adoue. "Mr. Rayner has rendered valuable service," the Galveston businessman told one brewery official, "for which we have paid regularly, not very liberally, it is true, and he has gotten additional small sums from other parties." But despite Rayner's usual tactic of leaving the amount of his compensation to the discretion of the brewers, they still occasionally grew impatient with his not-always-gentle reminders that he had to live off what they paid him. After recommending Rayner to an official of Anheuser-Busch, one of the Texas brewers suggested that Rayner had "one very, very serious drawback, however, and that is his mania for money. He will everlastingly and eternally be after you for the sinews of war." The "sinews of war" in reality did not amount to much. After the Travis County campaign Rayner submitted a statement of his expenses to the brewers, billing them $5.90 for railroad fare, $1 per day board, and $7.10 "for treating the boys down in the city, away from headquarters." For the six days' work he performed, Rayner told the brewers, "You can pay me what you please for the time." The brewers appear to have paid their black organizer a total of $50, including expenses—the equivalent of $900 in today's money—for his work in Austin. Even this sum was higher than usual, the normal reward being about half that amount. Brewers' Association records indicate that the most Rayner ever received in a year was $230 for an almost unbroken summer of campaigning in 1907.

Campaigning against prohibition both helped and hindered Rayner in his efforts to promote Conroe College. On one hand, most of the meaningful contributions to the school appear to have come from white antiprohibitionists. On the other hand, these contributions were never large, and time spent in politics was time that might have been devoted to fundraising. In the spring of 1907, after less than three years in his position at Conroe, Rayner's association with the school ended. Fire has since claimed the college's records, so the exact circumstances surrounding his departure cannot be stated with certainty. This much is known: at about the time Rayner left Conroe the school underwent a dramatic change, abandoning its original mission as a vocational college modeled after Tuskegee and becoming instead a theological school for the training of black ministers. The college affiliated itself with the one of Texas's black Baptist associations and hired Dr. David Abner, Jr., former president of Guadalupe College in Seguin, to replace Rayner as president. Abner brought with him from Guadalupe a corps of faculty members to teach religion.

Rayner may have resigned his position because of the accelerating rate at which prohibition elections were being called, or James Johnson may have decided that his fundraiser's increasingly high profile in politics was injurious to the school's interests. But the change in Conroe College's mission almost certainly played the major role in Rayner's departure. Since the 1880s the "Reverend" Rayner had shown little but contempt for other black preachers and organized religion in general. Near the end of his tenure at Conroe, the black leader wrote that the "army of bigots and fanatics" who comprised the forces of "religious conservatism" were so "vigilant in watching and guarding their creeds and traditions that they have no time to do good to any one. God never authorized any man or class of men to compile a creed." Drawing a curious analogy (given the writer's former status as a Populist platform committeeman), Rayner suggested that "creeds are to religion, what platforms are to political parties, a baited trap to catch the thoughtless, and increase the number of adherents. . . ." True Christians had only two creeds: "'Thou shalt love the Lord thy God with all thy heart, and with all thy soul, and with all thy mind' . . . . [and] 'Thou shall love thy neighbor as thyself.'"

Although baptized as a Baptist years before, Rayner had grown deeply disillusioned with organized religion. "Suppose I declare that the life and character of a Christian is God's only church on earth," he proposed in 1909. "A Christian can not be a sectarian, because a sectarian is a devotee to some ecclesiastical concoction boiled in the crucible of religious intolerance by high caste hierarchs." Striking blow after blow at the resurgent Protestant fundamentalism of the Progressive Era, Rayner articulated a philosophy of religion that reflected older, antebellum concepts of human perfectionism. He argued that there was "no such condition as human depravity; what we call depravity is simply the good spot in man concealed, and the true science of salvation is to know how to find this good spot and develop it." Rayner contended that "the evolution of thought is the revelation of God, and I believe I can be the son of God, just like Jesus the Christ was while he was in flesh."

Protestant Christianity historically had placed its greatest emphasis on personal salvation. While Rayner declared that humans could gain salvation by achieving perfection, such individual perfection was made possible only by working to reform society. The church, he wrote in 1909, should be "a corporation of givers and altruistic workers, who co-labor with Christ for the redemption of humanity." He was convinced that the time had come "for the people to know the great difference between Christianity and religion. . . . Christianity means personal service first, last, and all the time." Traditional black religion had placed much emphasis on the afterlife, and Rayner frequently argued that "Christianity is not a ticket to admit man into heaven, but an antidote for the love for sin. The heaven we create here is as beatific as the heaven hereafter." He acknowledged that blacks were making progress, but that progress was occurring "in spite of the churches." Continuing his lifelong criticism of the black clergy, he declared that "the preachers in my race talk too much about heaven, golden slippers, diamond crowns and long white robes, when they should be preaching about duty, means to make the best use of all industrial opportunities, and that efficient service means honesty, politeness, and obedience."

Formulating this secular, reformist theology enabled Rayner to reach into his own past and resurrect many of the old Populist doctrines without having to place them in a political context. As he had done in his Populist days, Rayner forcefully criticized the excesses of American capitalism. There was nothing inherently wrong in American democracy, private enterprise, or material wealth, he posited, but when democracy prostituted itself before the corporations, when pursuit of private interests conflicted with the common good, and when love of money was placed before love of family and fellow man, something had gone terribly wrong. So while Rayner accepted money from the brewers' cartel and pandered to the likes of John Henry Kirby, he also issued public indictments of capitalism, materialism, and greed. If he saw the contradiction in doing so, he kept it to himself.

"The dollar mania," Rayner warned, "is now a national epidemic," and he believed that the churches were largely to blame. Noting the frequent conflict between capitalism and Christian values, he lambasted the hypocrisy of pious monopolists: "The rich people make the church a large donation and then go out and organize a combine to corner the necessities of life, and expect God to help them rob the poor because of their gift to the church. Is this civilization? Is this Christianity?" America, its individualistic values reinforced by organized religion, had given the corporations carte blanche to exploit the poor. In the process, the nation's political institutions had been corrupted.

Rayner had sought to translate his beliefs about service to one's fellow man into action via Conroe College and had failed. The college's metamorphosis from a secular vocational school to a training ground for old-fashioned Baptist ministers must have come as a severe personal affront to the man who believed that "church power is the most sublime, the most drastic, the most intolerant and the most destructive of human liberties." In the four years following his departure from Conroe, Rayner was forced to rely on his political activities and journalistic efforts as outlets for his reformist urges. But in 1911 a new chance to help his race arose, and once more he seized the opportunity. In August of that year Rayner was appointed financial agent for the Farmers' Improvement Agricultural School at Ladonia in northeast Texas. Perhaps this time he would be able to realize his own vision of how the black race was to effect its own salvation.

The Farmers' Improvement Society (F.I.S.), which sponsored the school, was in 1911 the largest and most influential black self-help organization in Texas and perhaps the South. Founded in 1890 by Robert Lloyd Smith, a native of Charleston, South Carolina, and organized at a time when the Colored Farmers' Alliance was in decline, the F.I.S. was intended to encourage black solidarity and cooperation, teach black farmers to be more efficient and self-sufficient, and offer affordable insurance and burial benefits. It grew slowly at first, but by the time Rayner became affiliated with it the society boasted 800 branches with 12,000 members.

It comes as no surprise that Rayner and Smith would be attracted to one another, for the two men shared similar philosophies of black uplift. As a devoted friend and adherent of Booker T. Washington, Smith had faithfully sought to emulate Washington's strategies of self-help and accommodation. Yet, like Rayner, Smith was at the same time an active politician. Avoiding Populism, he had served as Texas's last black Republican state legislator from 1895 to 1899. At Booker T. Washington's urging, President Theodore Roosevelt had appointed Smith deputy to the U.S. marshal for eastern Texas in 1902, a position Smith had held until his removal by President William Howard Taft in 1909. Thus, like Rayner and many other black leaders in the early twentieth century, Smith seemingly espoused the accommodationist philosophy even while striving to preserve a measure of black political influence and working behind the scenes for racial justice.

Smith had long dreamed of an agricultural school as a natural complement to the other functions of the F.I.S. When the institution finally opened its doors in 1909, its stated purpose was threefold: "First: To give the student a practical training in correct methods of farming. Second: To give him a good, well-trained mind by pursuing a fair course of instruction at least as far advanced as the high school. Third: To train him up to true family life where habits of order, system, and thoroughness prevail." In other words, Smith's ideas about the kind of training blacks needed almost exactly matched those that Rayner had enunciated in 1904 and had sought to implement at Conroe College. Although Smith referred to the F.I.S. school as a college, it was really a boarding school for children from grades one through twelve. Like Conroe in its earlier days—and indeed like Tuskegee Institute—the F.I.S. school combined basic academic and vocational training with a strong dose of moral instruction. Conroe College and the Farmers' Improvement School had another thing in common; both were always on shaky financial ground. Local F.I.S. branches were supposed to contribute to the school's upkeep, but impoverished black farmers could never adequately support the institution. When Smith hired Rayner to oversee fundraising, the school owned eighty-two acres of sandy farmland, on which sat three buildings. As the school's new financial agent, Rayner immediately set out to publicize the cause and, hopefully, convince white Texans to contribute to it.

During the next three years Rayner dusted off all of his old techniques and renewed his former contacts in what was essentially a replay of his service to the Conroe school. He traveled far and wide across Texas, lecturing before both black and white audiences, and trying to cultivate the goodwill of anyone with money. He bombarded the newspapers with stories about the F.I.S. and its innovative program for black uplift. The school was crowded and desperately needed more buildings and equipment, but after reading the first of Rayner's publicity pieces in the *Galveston News*, Smith seemed confident "that at last we have found a man who can let the world know what we are trying to do." To this he soon added, "I hope that you will hustle as never before in all your days."

If possible, Rayner went to even greater lengths than he had in the Conroe days to ingratiate himself with powerful whites. One of his first acts as financial agent was to write a letter to J. S. "K. Lamity" Bonner, editor of *K. Lamity's Harpoon*, a bitingly satirical newspaper published in Austin. Bonner enjoyed a well-deserved reputation as the preeminent race-baiter in Texas, yet Rayner addressed him respectfully, agreeing that the racist editor had "well advertised the derelict negro" and meekly asking him to put in "a good word of commendation for the worthy negro." Bonner responded by defending his extreme racism and then presenting Rayner to his readers as "a worthy example for the negro race." What Rayner or the F.I.S. school gained from such an endorsement is at best questionable, but it must have come at a great psychological cost to the once-proud black leader.

Soon after accepting the F.I.S. position, Rayner reintroduced the idea of a Hall of Faithfulness to be financed by white donations in commemoration of the steadfast services rendered by southern slaves to the Confederacy during the Civil War. If Robert Smith objected to such a degrading tactic, he must have swallowed his pride, as Rayner had done long ago, and agreed that the end justified the means. Once again whites throughout the state applauded Rayner's accommodationist stance. One admirer declared that "Rayner is the most unselfish negro I ever knew" and pronounced him "the greatest negro on the American continent." Another wrote, "Not 200 miles from Houston an aged ex-slave resides. He is frequently called 'the white nigger.' At the risk of his life he stood by the whites during the crucial period of reconstruction, his work being like that of a mediator between the two races. To respect all in their several places and relations as superiors, inferiors, or equals is the solution of any social or race problem."

Years of telling whites the things they wanted to hear were beginning to take their toll on Rayner's store of personal dignity. In 1904 he had told stories about helping his white father hide valuables from the approaching Yankees; by 1912 these stories had become tales about "standing with the whites" during Reconstruction. While there was perhaps some truth in his "faithful slave" stories, Rayner was simply lying about his course during Reconstruction; he could never let it be known that he had been a Radical Republican officeholder. At times he had stooped even lower, telling various whites that he was "no admirer" of the social-equality-seeking Booker T. Washington and that he considered Thomas Dixon, author of racist novels such as *The Clansman*, to be "a wonderful writer and a deep and profound thinker." In trying to appeal to the rapidly disappearing paternalism of upper-class whites by emphasizing the class differences among blacks, he had succeeded primarily in making himself appear elitist. The many black people who once had idolized Rayner as a Populist orator must now have wondered how he could be so critical of common blacks, and other African American leaders often thought he simply went too far in trying to placate whites. A black newspaper editor seriously questioned Rayner's accommodationist course in these terms:

> The southern whites are not fools. They know every negro desires every right which the laws of the land guarantee him. They know the only reason he is not in possession of them is because he can not take them, and it is our opinion that they are without respect for the negro who talks to them contrarywise. Negroes of the Rayner brand should receive a welcome in neither race. The brave white men of the South, like brave men everywhere, loathe a coward, who, instead of battling for his liberties, whines like the whipped dog, or who, like a grinning jackass, declares that he deserves none.

The editor was mistaken about the "brave white men" who "loathed" a black sycophant; in reality, the more sycophantic a black man was, the more whites applauded him. Rayner's stature among whites testifies to this. But another of Rayner's black critics, Dallas minister A. S. Jackson, placed his condemnation of Rayner in a different context. Referring to the proposed Hall of Faithfulness, Jackson reportedly said that "no kind of building and school was worth the sacrifice of manhood that Raynor [sic] was making and that he would find that in trying to satisfy the white supremacists of Texas, he was attempting to feed a wolf—'the more you give him, the more he wants.'" Rayner gradually was discovering the cruel truth in Jackson's analysis. The more concessions he made to white supremacy, the more strident that white supremacy became. For black leaders in the Progressive Era, temporary sacrifices of principle had a way of becoming permanent losses. Nothing illustrates this better than Rayner's role in party politics at the start of the twentieth century.

# CHAPTER SIX
## The Price of Accommodation

DURING THE YEARS following the defeat of Populism, Rayner became a frequent contributor of essays and letters to the editor in major Texas newspapers. It is unknown whether he received pay for any of his writings, but they became a more-or-less regular feature in the *Houston Chronicle* and other papers. White newspapers might have hesitated to publish radical black-rights views, but Rayner had long since ceased to publish anything that might anger whites. Conservative editors seemingly delighted in showcasing the views of accommodating negroes like Rayner, who had grown adept at telling whites things they liked to hear. Still it was a way for the old Populist to maintain a public presence, and he apparently enjoyed the attention that his literary efforts brought him. It allowed him to believe that he still spoke for the "better sort" of black Texans, and to ensure that whites believed it as well.

In 1912 Rayner sat down to pen another essay for the *Chronicle*. Apparently reflecting on his own political career, he made what seemed to be a disarming confession:

> Since some of the colored race have attempted to be protagonist in politics, we (negroes) have been deceived by irridescent [sic] visions of political power and idle ease, and misled by utopian promises, and we (negroes) as a race became so hallucinated . . . that we could not see the red flag of danger ahead, and when we came to our senses we found

our political opportunities circumscribed, and our manhood proscribed, and what our fatuous presumption did in the past, our meekness and general moral worth must undo. The negro of today is not the negro of yesterday. Man must make himself worthy and admirable before he attempts by his vote to shape the policy and fix the destiny of states. . . . Politics has nothing to offer the negro.

Yet as Rayner's campaigning against prohibition has demonstrated, his public statements condemning black political participation cannot always be taken at face value. Indeed, his political interests after the turn of the century had not ended with local-option elections. He was still desperately searching for some meaningful political voice.

When Rayner had reentered public life in 1903, he not only went to work for Conroe College and campaigned against prohibition but he also sought once again to influence party politics. For all practical purposes the People's Party was gone by this time, and the state's Republicans had been almost as successful as the Democrats in purging their ranks of black participants. Disfranchisement had reduced the number of African American voters in Texas general elections from about 160,000 to somewhere between 15,000 and 40,000. Only in certain very close elections could blacks hold the balance of power as they had often done in the 1890s. Confronted with this set of circumstances, Rayner concluded that he would simply support the best candidate in any given race, regardless of party affiliation. That candidate might be an old Populist-turned-Democrat who had been a personal friend in the 1890s. He might be a Democrat who, if elected, would perhaps prove friendly to Rayner's school projects. Rayner sometimes supported a candidate who on racial issues was merely the lesser of two evils in a two-man race. And occasionally he lent his political weight to a campaign out of sheer self-interest. Usually several of these factors combined to convince the black politician to support a certain candidate. For an African American seeking to maintain some voice in politics, there was simply no such thing as a consistent course.

Such was the case in a 1903 congressional race, Rayner's first recorded political activity following the defeat of Populism. He campaigned in Houston's sizable black community on behalf of Democratic congressional candidate J. M. Pinckney, who was opposed by an unusually strong Republican nominee. A Confederate veteran from Waller County, Pinckney had earned a reputation as a friend to blacks while serving as district attorney and county judge. His antilynching utterances apparently canceled any objections that Rayner might have entertained because of Pinckney's stance as a prohibitionist and a Democrat. The campaign was unusual because of recent events involving the black community in Houston. In an effort to effect the repeal of a municipal ordinance that had recently segregated the city's streetcar system, a surprising number of the city's African Americans had paid their poll taxes and registered to vote; consequently they could also vote in the congressional election. With African American support, Pinckney carried Harris County by a slim margin, 974 votes to his Republican opponent's 950. In campaigning for Pinckney, Rayner obviously relinquished what had been his overriding goal in the Populist years: defeating the Democratic party at all costs.

This congressional race demonstrates Rayner's new-found willingness to support whatever candidate he deemed best. But Pinckney's mild antilynching stance fails to tell the entire story of why Rayner campaigned for a white Democrat. As it turns out, Rayner was seeking to be appointed superintendent of the State Colored Blind Asylum.

In Rayner's day, political patronage played a major role in the functioning of state government. Politicians won elections by promising state employment to loyal supporters, and men like Rayner who coveted such jobs worked hard to prove their value in elections. In this case, Rayner needed to pull strings with Democratic governor S. W. T. Lanham, and he somehow determined that a recommendation from the chairman of Pinckney's campaign committee would do the trick. Accordingly, following the election Rayner secured the desired letter of recommendation, which stated that there had "never been a time" when Rayner had failed to "strictly identify" with the political interests of whites. In the end, the governor did not name Rayner to the post, but the episode suggests that the former Populist had decided to use his political connections to further his own interests as well as those of his race. He had a wife and five children to support, and the state job would pay well. If securing it meant supporting a Democrat, so be it. On at least two other occasions Rayner tried to secure the appointment, but he never succeeded. Such sacrifices of principle—so unthinkable during the heyday of the Populist Revolt—would be depressingly commonplace for Rayner in the new century.

Rayner campaigned for a few other white Democrats over the years, most notably his old patron John Henry Kirby when the lumber baron ran successfully for the state legislature in 1912. Often they were potential contributors to Rayner's schools or men who would perhaps use their political influence to send some patronage Rayner's way. But in the two decades following the defeat of the Populists, Rayner more often than not supported the Republican Party. He publicly proclaimed that "in religion and politics" he was an independent, arguing that anyone who votes a straight party ticket "indirectly acknowledges that he allows others to do his own thinking." Rayner's independence naturally stemmed from his long-held antipathy toward the two major parties, but it also reflected the reality that blacks possessed few palatable political options after the turn of the century.

By the early 1900s what was left of the Republican Party in the South was divided into so-called Lily-White and Black-and-Tan factions, with the Lily-Whites generally dominant. As the name suggests, the Lily-Whites wanted to exclude blacks and remake the Republican Party into a conservative probusiness party, and the Black-and-Tans sought to maintain the old Reconstruction coalition that included African Americans in the party's ranks. Despite his public stance as an independent in politics, Rayner frequently came out in favor of the Republicans, invariably doing so in presidential elections. But as usual in his erratic political career, Rayner did not behave as one might expect. Incredibly, rather than support the Black-and-Tan faction of the Texas G.O.P., he urged acquiescence in Lily-White control of the state party! In language that would befit the whitest of Lily-White Republicans, he suggested that the only way to build up the party in the South was to place it under the leadership of southern whites. "Some facts must be admitted even if they are painful," Rayner wrote, "and one fact is: That the white man who associates with the negro on terms of political equality in Republican conventions in the South will not in these days be able to induce other white men to unite with the Republican party."

There was much truth in this analysis. The great stumbling block for the Republican party in the South always had been its reputation as the party of blacks. Indeed, time has shown that the establishment of the two-party system in the South depended on the reconstitution of the Republicans as a conservative probusiness party controlled by whites. The problem for Rayner was not that he misunderstood what must be done to revive the Republican Party; the problem was that his solution depended on the permanent removal of blacks from positions of party leadership. Was bringing two-party politics to the South worth such a sacrifice? Rayner concluded that it was. Thus in politics, as in education, he tried to "feed the wolf" of white supremacy by his willingness to support a Lily-White Republican Party. But instead of being thankful for black acquiescence in white leadership and, in return, championing basic black rights, the Republicans, now free of African American influence, simply ignored their interests. The more Rayner fed the wolf, the more it wanted.

Rayner held himself aloof from public participation in Republican politics until the elections of 1908. With the Lily-White faction now in control of the party, Rayner in August of that year advised blacks that "there is nothing for the political negro to gain by opposing the political methods of the white Republicans in Texas. . . ." In May 1908 Rayner contacted Cecil Lyon, a white Texas Republican leader supported by the Lily-Whites, offering his services as a stump speaker in the fall presidential campaign. The black orator wished to make a speaking tour of Illinois, Indiana, New York, Pennsylvania, and Maryland—states where a mobilized black vote might play a decisive role in bringing a Republican victory. The white Republican believed that Rayner had "absolutely the right idea" about the need for blacks to consent to white leadership of the party and promised Rayner to do anything he could to help arrange the tour, but he explained that any action would have to wait until the national committee met and devised a campaign plan. Lyon denied wanting "to run the negro out of the party." However, he pointed out that even if every black in Texas voted Republican, the party still could not carry state elections.

With his views now in harmony with those of the state party's white leader, Rayner was ready to work for the presidential election of William Howard Taft. The Taft campaign apparently never availed itself of Rayner's services, but Rayner continued to turn his pen and influence to the task of supporting the national Republican Party. As time went by though, the Texas Republican Party more fully embraced the Lily-White policy of exluding blacks altogether, and by 1910 Rayner had had enough. J. O. Terrell, the G.O.P. gubernatorial nominee, opened his campaign by proclaiming that "the Republican party in Texas would never be again dominated by an 'alien race.'" Rayner lashed out at the "ingratitude and prejudice" of Terrell, reminding his reading audience in the *Houston Chronicle* that despite "persuasion, intimidation, bribe and persecution, blacks had continued to vote Republican. Now the party was repaying black fidelity by branding them "aliens." Rayner could accept Republican support for suffrage restriction; he could endure white control of the party's conventions; he could concede the fruits of patronage to white Republicans; but he would never countenance the party's standard-bearer questioning the Americanism of blacks. "How can the negro be an alien," he asked angrily, "when he has been in America 291 years?" Furthermore, the black man had been "a brave soldier and a faithful servant in every war this country has engaged [in] from the 'Boston massacre' to San Juan Hill." Rayner concluded this public outburst by telling African Americans that they would be better off if the South remained Democratic. "There is a duty which the negro owes to his self-respect, greater than any duty he owes to any political party, and before he can vote for Mr. J. O. Terrell he will have to dishonor his self respect and the love he has for his race. The negro has made many political mistakes because he followed bad white men, but 'never more.

For the next two years Rayner felt so discouraged about the prospects for African Americans in politics that he often recommended that they eschew politics altogether. In early 1912 he stated that "the negro farmers in Texas have no confidence in political promises; they do not care if Hon. J. K. Vardaman secures the repeal of the thirteenth, fourteenth and fifteenth amendments to our national constitution, nor do they care if Mr. Vardaman repeals the ten commandments and burns up all the Bibles—God lives, and the negroes are trusting in righteousness of an all-wise and all powerful God." However, the key question facing Texas Republicans in the spring of 1912 was not the Mississippi demagogue, Vardaman, but rather the question of who was to be the party's presidential nominee. Taft and Roosevelt fought for control of the Republican Party, bitterly dividing it nationally and in Texas. By this time Rayner's essays in the *Houston Chronicle* had acquired something of a cult following among readers of both races. One of those readers submitted a series of questions to the black pundit, requesting for the benefit of the paper's readers that Rayner state his public position on current issues facing blacks.

In his reply Rayner voiced his clearest warning yet about the futility of black participation in partisan politics. Although he acknowledged that his words would cause many African Americans "to misunderstand and mistrust my council," Rayner nevertheless advised blacks "to keep out of the fight" and let the warring Republican factions "'stew in their own grease.'" With an indictment of the Republican Party reminiscent of his harangues from the Populist era, Rayner charged that "the Republican Party of today is simply sponsor for the powers that prey upon labor." The onetime party of Lincoln, he contended, now supports "the autocratic centralization of power in the national government, and believes that corporations are great individuals with immunities and greater privileges to do as they please." Republicans had "apotheosized the dollar, and made the voter an obsequious worshiper." Rayner's verdict echoed that of his early Populist days: "The Republican party in the South has nothing for the negro."

Despite these strictures concerning black participation in partisan politics, Rayner in 1912 made yet another exception to his own advice. Far from letting the Taft and Roosevelt factions "stew in their own grease," he vigorously took sides in favor of Taft and against the Democratic nominee Woodrow Wilson and third-party candidate Theodore Roosevelt, who was courting the Lily-White Republican vote in the South. Rayner composed an impassioned public letter bitterly denouncing Roosevelt as a "political maniac" who was "trying to organize a white man's Progressive party out of the Negro haters of the North and South," and urging blacks to vote for Taft. Assuming the persona of the Great Emancipator, Rayner entitled his anonymous appeal "The Spirit of Abraham Lincoln Calling His Colored Children Whom He Emancipated." Speaking through the persona of Lincoln, Rayner reminded African Americans that citizenship and the right to vote had "cost this Country streams of tears and blood; and great national pain and suffering." Failure to go the polls would be a sign of ingratitude; in effect, blacks would be saying that they wished "to return to a slavery more debasing than chattel slavery." He ordered blacks to go to the polls on election day and vote a straight Republican ticket. "The whole world is watching you," he stated. "The spirits of John Brown and Abraham Lincoln will be at every ballot box in Texas on the day of election in next November to see if the colored man is true to the party that gave him liberty, the right to vote, and the free school. God save the colored people from Democratic hate and wicked persecution is the prayer of Abraham Lincoln."

The "Spirit of Abraham Lincoln" essay was, of course, an anonymous essay; in his signed, public essays—especially those in the white press—Rayner continued to advise blacks to shun politics. In 1912 such advice included warnings against black participation in the prohibition issue. "There once was a time," he wrote, "when the question of prohibition could be discussed without passion," but now "both sides have exhausted their store of reason and facts, and have also exhausted their patience, and from now on all local option elections will be force meet force, and it will be best for all negro voters to keep away from the polls on all local option elections." The man who had spent years urging blacks to vote against prohibition now told them to "let the white people settle this question among themselves." It had grown "too dangerous for the negro voter to dive into."

Rayner clearly felt embittered about the failure of white men from both parties and from both sides of the prohibition question to further the cause of black voting rights. But it must be remembered that he was writing for a newspaper with a large white readership and that his main public cause at the time was fundraising for the F.I.S. school. In fact, Rayner's private actions again directly contradicted his public advice to blacks in the *Chronicle*. A few weeks later he was in Beeville at the behest of the brewers, holding a "secret caucus" with black leaders, showing them how to mark their ballots in the upcoming local-option election, and laboring to "set in motion some subtle forces which would get the colored voters to the polls."

Over the next two years Rayner's public political utterances grew even more erratic and contradictory. He adhered to his belief that blacks should "keep out of conventions and let the white people manage the political campaigns," but beyond this he appeared unable to decide what they should do. At times he advised African Americans "to vote with the Southerner on all questions" and praised Democrats such as John H. Kirby and Joe Eagle, but then he turned around and complained that there was "no relief in politics." He wrote in the *Chronicle* that blacks should be "neutral in political campaigns" and "vote for the best man," and then he proceeded to inform his readers that he would "vote that Republican ticket of the Old Abraham Lincoln stamp." Rayner had tested virtually every political option since the demise of Populism, and none seemed to hold any promise for betterment of the race. The rich promise of the 1890s was now nothing but a distant memory. It is true that much of the apparent irrationality of his course stemmed from the need to stay in the good graces of the brewers and to appear apolitical in his role as financial agent of the Farmers' Improvement school. And of course he had to keep food on his family's table.

Rayner's years in the public spotlight were rapidly drawing to a close by the mid-1910s. When his benefactor Bertrand Adoue died in late 1911, Rayner knew he had lost his "most substantial friend" from the ranks of the antiprohibitionists. Rayner's relationship with the brewers had always been a stormy one, for although he left his pay to their discretion, the beermakers considered their black organizer greedy. While alive, Adoue had played the peacemaker, pointing out Rayner's value to the cause and reminding the brewery officials that he had not been paid very generously. In July 1912, however, when Rayner approached the brewers' representative Otto Wahrmund for an F.I.S. donation following a successful local-option election, the brewer turned him down, claiming to be too busy. Rayner's quick temper, which he normally held in check when dealing with white people, overruled his patience. He fired an irate letter back to Wahrmund:

> You say you have not the time to help me is a sad surprise. I am a protagonist in the cause of anti-prohibition. I have done more anti-prohibition than all the other _____ [sic] combined. I have placed the iron hand of Machiavel[l]ian diplomacy upon the religious, educational and business gatherings of my people and kept them from making campaign thunder for the intolerant and fanatical prohibitionists. I have wet a score of dry counties in Texas or kept them from drying. I merit the highest consideration from the patriotic antis. I represent the colored farmers of Texas, and I tell you their votes saved the State from the blighting hand of the prohibitionists. . . . How can you . . . ignore my importunities? Every saloon in San Antonio should donate to my school. I have stood undaunted before the frowns of religious women and endured the imprecations of mad prohibitionists and have been forced to lose personal property and mortgage the best of my property . . . and my endurance and suffering has been your material progress. I am now doing all I can to make the colored pastors of your city your political friends. You say "you will have to excuse me," I will do so but when you need a colored vote and call on me I shall need tell you to excuse me. . . . I am not a renegade; but if you all want success you can have it through my labors. I am a man, and I am as proud of my influence as you are of your great wealth and prosperous business. Can you forgive a slight or ignore it? I know my powers, and you know yourself, and when you slight my powers it proves that you don't need mine. Don't trouble to answer this letter. You "have not the time to spare."

Rayner thus parted ways with the brewers amid great resentment on both sides. Less than three years later the state attorney general hauled the Texas Brewers' Association and the individual breweries who composed the cartel into district court and charged them with antitrust violations and illegal interference in elections. The trial resulted in a resounding defeat for the beermakers, who were fined $281,000 and forfeited their charters to conduct business in Texas. Ironically, the state's case rested primarily on subpoenaed records of the brewers, and among the most damning of the evidence was the extensive correspondence between the brewery officials and their black political organizer. In the eyes of white Progressive Democrats, the brewers simply seemed to be using Rayner to manipulate the black vote—a practice that harkened back to the old days of corrupt nineteenth-century Texas politics. Considering the strained relations between himself and the brewers, Rayner could not have helped feeling a certain satisfaction as the brewers' empire collapsed around them.

The brewers' refusal to contribute to the F.I.S. school was indicative of Rayner's general failure to produce the major donations the institution needed. In a replay of his experiences at Conroe, the considerable publicity Rayner achieved for the school was never matched by financial support from those who applauded the loudest. Attempts to tap northern philanthropy via Booker T. Washington and Tuskegee Institute met with only limited success. Sometime in mid-1914 Rayner left the Farmers' Improvement Society. Records of the circumstances surrounding his departure have not survived, but it is almost certain that a combination of declining health, personal financial difficulties, and his lack of major successes as a fundraiser prompted the move.

With his final retirement from active public life, Rayner found it increasingly difficult to support himself and his family in the middle-class style to which they were accustomed. It is true that by 1914 the Rayners had managed to accumulate eight lots in the black section of Calvert, on which John maintained rented houses. In addition the family had purchased a small farm in the country, also rented to a tenant. After his retirement Rayner and his sons maintained the property and from time to time he collected rents on land owned by white absentee landlords in return for a percentage of the monies collected. When these sources of income proved insufficient, he fell back on his longtime patron, John H. Kirby, for employment. Kirby's East Texas lumber mills employed both black and white laborers, and occasionally the timber king needed additional hands. With his considerable powers of persuasion and far-flung contacts in the African American communities of Texas, Rayner could easily procure all the mill hands Kirby needed. In the last several years of his life Rayner performed this service on an irregular basis, and at one point he also recruited Mexican peasants to work in the mills. In a career filled with irony, perhaps the most tragic example was the manner in which he was forced to make a living in his last years. As a Populist, the black orator had spent years championing the tenant farmer and denouncing landlords, absentee owners, and greedy corporations. Now Rayner himself was something of a landlord, assisted absentee owners, and recruited hundreds of poor workers into the hands of a large corporation.

As Rayner's reliance on Kirby grew, he adopted an increasingly conservative political posture in his dealings with the lumber magnate, partly because Kirby himself had gradually changed from conservative to reactionary in politics. The "Prince of the Pines," however, remained paternalistic in his dealings with Rayner, and the black politician felt he had no choice but to cultivate the relationship. Kirby's feelings about Rayner were unquestionably sincere; he never failed to answer his black friend's letters promptly and personally, and he wrote privately to a white friend of his "abiding respect" for the "colored preacher, teacher and scholar."

How much of Rayner's conservatism in his letters to Kirby was genuine and how much was a sham cannot be determined for sure. But clearly the two men sincerely concurred in their mutual hatred of the "reformers" in the progressive wing of the Democratic party, albeit for different reasons. "We are living in an inauspicious age," Rayner confided to Kirby in July 1915. He criticized the "greed of labor unions" and "the anarchy of agrarianism," sentiments that the millionaire lumber baron surely would have endorsed. One suspects, however, that Kirby would have only shook his head at Rayner's prediction that "some day the Negro vote will be called upon to save the South" from the demagoguery of progressive reformers.

Even Kirby's sponsorship fell short of providing enough income for Rayner to meet his financial obligations. In 1914 his money troubles were compounded by a fire that completely destroyed one of his rental houses. When the fire broke out, Calvert's new fire truck "made a record run" to the scene, but the city had not bothered to extend water mains into the segregated neighborhood. The house was a total loss. As he fell behind in his taxes, Rayner resorted to more desperate measures. Now he approached wealthy Houston businessman Harris Masterson for an $800 loan. A former Republican judge who had amassed a fortune in land, Masterson extended the loan, assuming a mortgage on Rayner's eight town lots, including the family's home. The sum was to be paid with interest in six months. When the due date arrived, Rayner could not produce the sum. He pleaded for more time, which Masterson granted. By January 1915, four months after the payment was due, the money still had not materialized, and Masterson foreclosed. Unbeknownst to her husband, Clarissa Rayner penned a desperate letter to Masterson:

> Dear Sir, My husband had you to take up some notes here in the bank on our property and the notes would have been paid but we did not get enough rent on our farm to pay the notes. I worked so hard to buy the property that you have a mortgage on and I don't want to lose my property and beg you to have mercy and patience with us and give us more time. If you please, let me know if you will give us some more time. We will pay you interest for all the time we use you[r] money. I am the wife of J.B. Rayner. Will you please let me hear from you?

Three more months passed, and Masterson neither had sold the property nor evicted the Rayners. His agent wrote to Rayner, offering him a chance to buy back the property (despite the fact that the black leader had "acted very bad" and shown himself "to be ungratefull and unapreciative [sic] and unreliable"). At the last moment Rayner somehow managed to buy back his own house and the lot on which it stood, for an undisclosed amount. It is safe to say that

Masterson lost no money on the transaction. In the wake of this near-disaster, Rayner, reflecting on years spent in the poorly paying pursuits of politics and essay-writing, ruefully told Kirby that "I have been too zealous to get my people to '*think*,' and today my family is paying the tax for my past zeal."

Despite the financial troubles that occupied much of his attention in his last years, Rayner still found time to satisfy his insatiable appetite for reading, especially in contemporary sociological and scientific works. In the early 1910s Rayner's curiosity about history, race, and social reform brought him into contact with the flourishing eugenics movement that had emerged in the United States in the early twentieth century. Extensive studies in criminal anthropology and a simplistic understanding of modern genetic theory convinced many reform-oriented Americans that crime, vice, feeblemindedness, alcoholism, poverty, and disease were hereditary rather than products of a faulty environment. Racists pressed the new theories into service to explain the alleged deficiencies of African Americans, and nativists did the same in regard to new immigrants. By about 1910 various societies and individuals were promoting eugenics-inspired measures such as immigration restriction and sterilization of the unfit—ideas the Nazis would later enthusiastically embrace.

Eugenics attracted Rayner for several reasons. First, it was "scientific," which appealed to Rayner's belief in the primacy of reason over emotion. Second, the emphasis on heredity helped him to explain why reform seemed to have failed in improving the moral and material progress of his people. However, eugenics was not just a negative movement aimed at preventing the unfit from outnumbering the fit; the school of thought also sought to facilitate the careful selection of biologically compatible mates, to encourage health, hygiene, and morality among parents, and to promote better prenatal care and child-rearing practices.

The movement's dualistic nature accommodated itself easily to Rayner's own complex mix of conservatism and reform-mindedness. Leaving further and further behind the egalitarianism of his Populist years, he began to stress the innate inequality of man, but he refused to let that belief diminish his fervor for reform. "All men are worthy," he pronounced, "but men are not equal, and the inequality of man is the axle upon which the restless wheel of evolution turns man continually toward the perfect and sublime." Rayner proposed in 1914 that "the mission of law is to adjust the inequality of man, and give to the weak and the humble an aegis of protection. . . ." But eugenics theory confirmed his growing suspicion that there were severe limits to reform. One could "take the red neck and hillbilly. . . ," he speculated, "and give him an immaculate and empyrean family and give him the most polished education, and when he reaches manhood he will be only a parrot—he can only repeat what he has learned from books, but cannot initiate nor originate."

In his writings on eugenics, Rayner reflected the competing strains of thought within the movement as well as his own inner conflict regarding the heredity versus environment argument. Although he believed "that man can obtain the transcendental perfect," he nonetheless thought that "civilization must have a base, a sure foundation, and this base must be uncontaminated blood corpuscles whose purity will be ambrosial food for the brain cells. When the blood is sin poisoned with filth the brain cells will be paralyzed and the will power destroyed." As a consequence, Rayner urged that "all diseased people and children of drunkards must be sterilized and the saloons closed up forever." If the contradiction between this pronouncement and his work on behalf of the brewers bothered him, he gave no indication of it.

While he was associated with the F.I.S. school, Rayner claimed that eugenics principles were being taught there. In this regard his beliefs in eugenics typified the positive rather than the negative aspects of the movement. When publicizing the school, he explained that "the girls are taught a knowledge of eugenics, how to understand prenatal influence, and the constructive and destructive influence of environment in motherhood." It was an odd combination of hereditarianism and environmentalism, therefore, that led him to recommend that pregnant women "see nothing but beauty, hear nothing but music and lovable truths, and [be] treated with immaculate reverence and celestial kindness. . . ." All the education in the world would be for naught if these influences were missing. After leaving the school, Rayner tried to convince Kirby to send him to the East Texas sawmill towns to lecture on eugenics to the black millworkers. Kirby agreed that it would be a good idea, but he claimed inability to finance the effort.

Rayner's growing skepticism about the ability of man to adapt and improve ultimately manifested itself not only in an embrace of eugenics but also of nativism. In a truly ironic twist of fate, the same ideology that had propelled the father into the Know-Nothing movement now captivated the son sixty years later. Twentieth-century blacks, of course, had greater justification for their resentment of immigrants than did antebellum white southerners. It was understandably difficult for African Americans to see the logic, or the justice, in allowing illiterate, recently arrived non-English-speaking immigrants to take their seats in a first-class railroad car while a southern-born, college-educated black had to make his way to the segregated second-class compartment. As Rayner put it, "the majority of the negroes may be incompetent voters, but when it comes to pure devotion to Americanism and an inextinguishable love for the South . . . the negro will be given the first place of honor by all who are competent to think."

Rayner employed nativism to underscore the blatant denial of meaningful citizenship to African Americans. "Our American civilization is very rapidly becoming Europeanized," he warned in 1914, "not from the castles of Europe, but from the hovels. . . . People whose ancestors never raised their hands in defense of liberty can not teach the sons of patriotic heroes lessons in freedom." Among those sons of patriots, of course, were African Americans like himself. He took pains to point out that the first blood shed in the Revolution was that of an African American, Crispus Attucks, and that Alexander Hamilton's mother was a mulatto. Himself the tax-paying grandson of a Revolutionary War veteran, it burned him that he was barred from voting in the Democratic primary in his own home town. If blacks were effectively denied the vote, he bitterly reasoned, so should recent immigrants be.

When the United States officially entered World War I in 1917, Rayner sensed a new opportunity for blacks. He long had opposed imperialism and war in general, but like other Americans he patriotically supported the war once the nation was engaged in it. Rayner guessed that if blacks could serve in combat roles, they would return from Europe with enhanced leverage to bargain for civil rights. Military service also would provide steady employment and encourage savings among young black males—goals he had spent years promoting. A week after Congress declared war on Germany, Rayner wrote to John Henry Kirby, expressing his opinion that blacks should be urged to serve. Apparently he wanted the lumber baron to send him to the mill towns to encourage enlistments. Rayner's letter has not been located, but Kirby's answer survives. "I do not agree with you," the Houstonian responded, "that they [blacks] can render the best service to their country at this time by seeking military positions. What our Republic needs and what the world needs is more producers." Kirby suggested that Rayner could serve the country best "by encouraging industry and patient and energetic toil in the lines for which your people are best qualified," and he refused to finance the ex-Populist's lectures promoting military enlistment in the mill towns.

Rayner replied by telling his benefactor that although Kirby had "righteous" motives, "the truculent enemies of the colored people say just what you say." Kirby would never do anything to hurt blacks intentionally, Rayner believed, but he had to disagree with the businessman's analysis of the situation. "Now when it comes to war," the black leader contended,

> I don't believe in its *"hell"* . . . I truly hope and pray that this country will never be forced to place a gun or sword in the colored man's hands. The sword is the sceptre of tyran[n]ical autocracy, the instrument of religious intolerance, and fanaticism, and I am perfectly willing for the white man to have a fee simple title to use it as long as the fatherhood of the Devil prevents the brotherhood of man. I believe in peace, virtue, toil, and plenty; and I truly desire all colored people to be Christlike in character, and to serve in truth and love all humanity. . . . I am still preaching, lecturing, and writing about the beauty, utility, peace, and prosperity of the farm life, and the hellish horrors of modern warfare:

but I will not teach my people an unpatriotic lesson. I tell my people if the country calls for you to go on the battle field, to go, and face the enemy and never retreat and never surrender.

Rayner did not live to see the end of the war, and the great majority of blacks who served their nation did so not in combat but in support capacities as stevedores, cooks, and manual laborers. He did survive long enough to read the news from Houston in September 1917, where, after continually being harassed by police and insulted by white citizens, black troops from Camp Logan staged a riot in which seventeen whites died. In the aftermath of the incident, thirteen black soldiers were hanged and forty-one given life sentences. African American participation in the war effort—far from bringing progress in black civil rights—seemed instead to fan the flames of prejudice. It was the same tired song that had been played and replayed since emancipation: black hopes were built up, only to be torn down. And the end result always was that whites rededicated themselves to keeping African Americans "in their place."

America's entry into World War I coincided with the onset of serious physical problems for Rayner. Over the years his stout physique had given way to overweight, and grueling years on the campaign trail and lecture circuit, with the inevitable bad food and insufficient rest, had taken their toll. Now sixty-seven years old, he confided to Kirby that he still had "to hustle for bread when not laboring for others," but that hustling was growing more difficult. All of his children were grown and gone from home. Despite Rayner's public efforts to keep blacks out of the cities and down on the farm, two of his sons had gone to Chicago—a move that Rayner had encouraged. His youngest daughter, Susie, was attending the colored normal school eighty miles away at Prairie View. Although he was a loving husband and a proponent of women's suffrage, John could be dictatorial around the house, demanding his meals served on time and hot. He had always maintained an office in his home, and he would not tolerate interruptions as he worked or wrote. With John's travels increasingly restricted by declining health and his sources of income more uncertain than ever, he and Clarissa took as many as five black children into their home as boarding students, with John as teacher.

In 1918 Rayner began to exhibit signs of what was probably either kidney or liver failure. Diagnosed as "dropsy," the illness resulted in edema, manifested as a massive swelling of the hands and feet. Confined mostly to his home, the dying politician could do little besides give his boarding students their lessons, help his less literate neighbors write letters and untangle minor legal affairs, and reflect on a lifetime spent battling white supremacy. Rayner never kept a diary, and almost no truly personal letters survive, but it seems that he had few genuinely close friends. His light skin, refined manners, polished speech, and close associations with whites had always set him apart from the majority of the blacks in Calvert. His last days apparently were very lonely.

Fortunately for the biographer, Rayner did bequeath one remarkable group of private writings to posterity. In the final years of his life he began compiling a collection of his own "Wise Sayings." This group of aphorisms, totaling more than 100 manuscript pages, appears originally to have been intended for publication, just like the rest of his essays. Indeed, certain of the sayings did find their way into print. But clearly the great majority of these adages were never published. They took the form of aphorisms because they undoubtedly were meant to be instructive and easy to remember. Never a philosopher in the sense of one who develops theories for their own sake, he had always intended that his essays, letters, and speeches educate and motivate his audiences to direct action. The theorist who never tried to put his ideas into practice had "exploited humanity from time immemorial," Rayner believed. Such a man was no better than the "practical man" whose only question was "'Will it pay?'" What appears to have happened is this: as he tried to put onto paper his innermost beliefs for the benefit of his readers, Rayner found that many of those beliefs expressed much more radical ideas than were permissible in the public press. Therefore he collected only the most "inoffensive" of the sayings for publication, but continued to write whatever he felt, strictly for his own benefit.

These adages cover a wide range of topics. Religion, education, war, money, marriage, and music all receive attention. Aphorisms are by definition simplistic, but they nevertheless serve as a convenient means of summarizing the writer's beliefs; Rayner's display a continuing interest in eugenics and dedication to nativism, but even stronger are the marks of his undying commitment to a Populistic conception of economics and materialism. "Commercialism," he wrote in one of them, "is a euphemistic word for artful preying: its motive is lustful covetousness, and it deals and exploits without a conscience or compunction." The religious emphasis, so prominent in the thought of southern Populists, emerges clearly in these writings: "The inordinate love for money, and ambition for power, are twin evils; whose father is Satan, and whose mother is selfishness." A number of the sayings were derived directly from the Populist diagnosis of the American economic system's ills: "When wealth concentrates, misery radiates." "No man can be charitable with money for which he did not give value received." "Interest on money invalidates the principal [sic] in man." "The man who takes usury from his fellow man, gives the devil a mortgage on his soul." "[Industrialist/philanthropist Andrew] Carnegie has erected many mausoleums for dead thought, and our economic system which enabled him to erect these sepulchral monuments keeps the people who produced his wealth from having time to read the books in the Carnegie Library."

The most prominent theme in the aphorisms, however, is not materialism. Not surprisingly, Rayner devoted much of the private thought of his last days to the question that had occupied his life—the relationship between the black and white races in America. These are the writings that were never published and that could not be published in the South of 1918. He put forward the main theme of the racial aphorisms in an absolutely straightforward manner: "God does not intend for one part of his people to feel that they are superior to another part." A number of the adages attack the hypocrisy of whites and the irrationality of racism. Rayner was particularly frustrated by the unending stream of white criticism of black intelligence and character. He pointed out that "the man or men who take from me the responsibilities of a full fledge[d] citizen, take from me the opportunity to prove the true mettle of my virtues." He continued in this vein by calling the white southerner "the most unreasonable of all men," because he "teaches the Negro to believe himself an inferior being, and at the same time requires of the Negro a character par excellent." If whites were superior, how was miscegenation to be explained? "A superior race never mixes their blood with the blood of an inferior race," Rayner reasoned. "How can you boast of your superiority," he asked, "when the world sees every day in the variegated complexion of the so called inferior race, the fruits of your most intimate social equality association with your so called inferior race?"

Since the Populist period, Rayner frequently had indulged in speculation about the future. In these private writings, his predictions assume an ominous, at times apocalyptic, vision. As a point of departure he noted that "time will prove whether the white man's civilization is *igni fatuus* or promethean fire whose celestial heat welds humanity into Christian solidarity." Yet he never completely relinquished his faith in the American system of government. As badly as things had turned out for blacks in the South, the root values of American civilization nevertheless were "all the light the Negro has in the night of intolerance," Rayner suggested. It was "dark now," but perhaps "the hideous and horrible travail of the Negro through the valley of political and industrial intolerance" would signal "the birth of the day." However, Rayner was terribly pessimistic about the coming days, and he issued some dire warnings to whites. "The white race can only save itself by saving the black race," he cautioned. "If the Southerner keeps his sentiments, he will be sure to lose his land, his political power, and be eliminated from the commercial affairs of the country. The aging writer believed that white supremacy would "finally be [the white man's] undoing, because the Southern white man is impinging a law that no man wrote, and no legislative body enacted." If the white man continued to nurse his "hallucinated idea of race superiority," he would awake one day to find that he was watching "through a retrospective kaleidoscope his superiority in the past."

The very words "superiority" and "inferiority" took on new meanings in Rayner's sayings. The superior man was merely "he who does his duty because he fears God and loves man." Conversely, "the most inferior man in the world is he who can not see his opportunity to do good." "The superior man," Rayner proposed, "labors to make all men superior, and the inferior man is he who is afraid to divide his opportunities with others. Again, the superior man is he who makes a righteous use of power." To the old Populist hero, whites clearly had failed to use their power righteously. The unreasoning prejudice that sanctioned the lynching and burning of blacks would discredit southern whites in the eyes of future generations. "The white people who say the most cruel things about the Negro," he declared, "are not morally nor mentally competent to write or express a thought that the future will pay any attention to." He reminded himself "never to listen to the counsel of the man who is too cowardly to contend for you to have equal political and industrial opportunities." Only when whites developed "intelligence and virtue enough to have mutual confidence in each other, respect for law, and a profound reverence for our course of justice," would mobs cease to "organize to murder and burn human beings." White southerners had forgotten one simple truth: "Only the tried are convicted, or cleared."

Turning his attention to the political institutions that undergirded the system of white supremacy, Rayner harshly indicted the Democratic Party. White southerners had imbued the party with a near-sacred infallibility, with tragic results. "The faith the South has in the Democratic party," he bitterly noted, was "stronger than the faith the South has in God." Throughout American history, every time whites had faced a struggle, blacks had been there "with strong arm and obedience, striking for the same." Each time whites "had resisted tyranny and fought for liberty the Negro was there with his gun fireing [sic] at every opportunity. . . ." Now whites had "monopolized all the good in the civilization which the Negro helped to build up," and it seemed to Rayner that blacks' only justice would come in some distant time and place, "where the 'Tree of Life' will not be guarded with Democratic sentinels."

But the Democratic sentinels would not even allow John B. Rayner to die in peace. Sometime in the last months of his life, he collided one last time with the local symbol of white supremacy, Calvert's town marshal. Ailing from dropsy and barely able to get around,

Rayner had failed to comply with a town ordinance requiring that pets be tagged. The white sheriff demanded that he tag his dog, and the black leader stubbornly refused. The angry lawman resorted to a time-honored southern remedy for dealing with its "uppity" blacks: physical violence. The beating he administered to Rayner was not particularly severe, but the victim was a sick man approaching sixty-eight years of age. After the assault, Rayner continued to see to his teaching duties as best he could, but gradually his condition deteriorated. In the "wise sayings," he had noted that as "our bodies gro[w] old, ugly, full of pains, and decrepted [sic], the soul is in travail, and will soon throw off its body and re-appear more like its Creator." On July 14, 1918, Rayner died of congestive heart failure. In keeping with his wishes, there was no church funeral. The family held a simple service in his home, and few of the newspapers for which he had once written bothered to note his passing. The next day he was laid to rest in the segregated cemetery on the outskirts of Calvert.

# Epilogue

THERE IS LITTLE THAT ONE CAN CALL encouraging in the story of John B. Rayner, for it is mostly a story of injustice, failure, and the humiliation of a man whose lifelong efforts to do good met with repeated frustration—primarily because of the distorting power of racism. Yet Rayner's life story is instructive because it reminds us of the sheer irrationality of that racism. Had he been born the legitimate son of Kenneth Rayner—minus the one-eighth or one-sixteenth African American heritage that made him "black" in the eyes of society—how dramatically different his life would have been. The world will always need people of John B. Rayner's talents and energy, but the United States of the late nineteenth and early twentieth centuries had little use for him. The ideology of white supremacy condemned him to a life on the margins of American society. In the end it robbed him of most of his personal dignity and forced him to compromise many of his cherished ideals. He died lonely, discouraged, and forgotten.

It did not have to be that way. Rayner came of age during the noble experiment of Radical Reconstruction, and he experienced firsthand the attempt at biracial democracy that briefly flourished in the 1870s. That experiment foundered on the rocks of racism and the lingering sectional hostilities of the Civil War, but in the 1890s an even more promising political movement—Populism—gave new hope that America might put aside its old sectional and racial animosities and move toward a new era of democratic cooperation between the races. Few images speak as clearly to the possibilities inherent in Populism than that of John B. Rayner standing on a speaker's platform in Houston's Market Square, surrounded by an ocean of black and white faces as he denounced monopolistic corporations and exposed the corruption of the two major political parties, stopping now and then to dress down white hecklers, secure that his white Populist brethren would personally step in to defend him if necessary.

The combined power of the two major parties and the entrenched racism of American society doomed Populism to defeat, and the remainder of Rayner's life story was one beset by ever-narrowing options. The last of his years coincided with perhaps the lowest point in American race relations since the days of slavery. Rayner had learned too late that the accommodation of white supremacists was as fruitless as black militancy, and it was a lesson that he had learned at a terrible cost to his pride and psyche. By the time of his death he could only express his true feelings about the injustices of American life by sitting in his home and writing bitter compositions that nobody else would see until historians discovered them in his papers some fifty years later.

The one thing that Rayner could have taken great pride in—had he lived longer—was the fate of his descendants. His three sons, Ivan Edward, Loris Melikoff, and Ahmed Arabi, moved to Chicago in the great black migration prior to 1920. Ahmed and Loris became undertakers and the funeral business that Ahmed founded remains in the family today. Its remarkable success has placed the Rayner family at the pinnacle of Chicago's African American community.

Rayner would have taken particular pride in the career of one of his grandsons. A. A. "Sammie" Rayner, Jr., served his country with the famed Tuskegee Airmen in World War II and then entered politics in Chicago in the early 1960s. Fiercely independent, he mounted serious but unsuccessful races for Congress four times and mayor of Chicago once. He also ran as an independent candidate for city alderman in 1963 and 1964, losing by narrow margins. But as black activist Stokely Carmichael noted of Sammie Rayner, "he was building an image in the black community as one who could and would speak out. The black people were getting the message." Rayner's difficulty in winning his first two city races was attributable to one basic fact: he was running in opposition to the corrupt machine politics of Mayor Richard Daley and against machine-backed candidates.

In 1967 Sammie Rayner mounted one final race for the city council. Chicago's Sixth Ward was an inner-city black neighborhood that had always been controlled by the machine. The candidate campaigned day after day, door to door, attending black civic functions and talking with the youth gangs on their own turf. On election day he won handily, becoming the first black to win a seat on the council by opposing the Democratic machine. But after his retirement from politics, Sammie Rayner disliked being identified as Chicago's first black anti-Daley alderman. "I wasn't anti-Daley," explained, "I was pro-people." His Populist grandfather would have approved.

*Feeding the Wolf: John B. Rayner and the Politics of Race, 1850–1918*
Developmental editor: Andrew J. Davidson
Copy editors: Andrew J. Davidson and Lucy Herz
Production editor: Lucy Herz
Cover design: DePinto Graphic Design
Printer: Versa Press, Inc.